Traditional
SOUTH
AFRICAN
Cooking

Traditional
SOUTH
AFRICAN
Cooking

MAGDALEEN VAN WYK & PAT BARTON

Published in 2007 by Struik Publishers
(a division of New Holland Publishing (South Africa)
(Pty) Ltd)
Cornelis Struik House, 80 McKenzie Street, Cape Town 8001
86–88 Edgware Road, London, W2 2EA, United Kingdom
Unit 1, 66 Gibbes Street, Chatswood, NSW 2067, Australia
218 Lake Road, Northcote, Auckland, New Zealand

www.struik.co.za

New Holland Publishing is a member of Avusa Ltd

Originally published as *A Taste of Tradition* 1994
Published as *Traditional South African Cooking* 1996, 1999
This edition 2007
2 3 4 5 6 7 8 9 10
Text © Magdaleen van Wyk and Pat Barton 1996
All photographs © Images of Africa/
Anthony Johnson 1996,
except pages 8/9 © The Argus;
page 32/33 © Foodpix/Photo Access;
page 40/41 © Alain Proust;
page 104/105 © Index Stock/Photo Access;
page 112/113 © Walter Knirr and
page 118/119 © Herman Potgieter

Publishing Manager: Linda de Villiers
Managing Editor: Cecilia Barfield
Editors: Sandie Vahl, Thea Coetzee (1994) and Irma van Wyk (2007)
Designer: Janine Damon
Cover: Beverley Dodd
Photographer: Anthony Johnson
Food Stylist: Vo Pollard
Assistant Stylist: Petal Palmer

Reproduction by Hirt & Carter Cape (Pty) Ltd
Printed and bound by Craft Print International Pte Ltd, Singapore

ISBN 978-1-77007-407-1

Over 40 000 unique African images available to purchase from our
image bank at www.imagesofafrica.co.za

IMAGES OF AFRICA
P H O T O L I B R A R Y

CONTENTS

ACKNOWLEDGEMENTS

The authors would like to thank Flesch Financial Publications for permission to use material from *Leipoldt's Cape Cookery*, Faldela Williams for material from *The Cape Malay Cookbook*, and Renata Coetzee for material from *The South African Culinary Tradition* and *Funa*.

The photographer, stylist and publishers would like to thank the following persons and companies in Cape Town for the crockery and material which they so kindly supplied:

Bric-a-Brac Lane, Claremont
Clarewood Antiques and Interiors, Claremont
Clementina van der Walt, Paarl
Fabric Library
Med Blue, Glencairn
Peter Visser Interiors
The Potter's Shop, Kalk Bay
Val Prout, Franschhoek
Wendy Hofmeyer, Rondebosch
Sylvia Grobbelaar, Oranjezicht

INTRODUCTION

Modern South Africans are fortunate to have a rich culinary heritage, built up from the cuisines of many different nations. While no dish can be said to be peculiarly South African, the subtle adaptation of these 'imported' recipes in the addition of local ingredients and the introduction of innovative cooking methods have made for an original cuisine.

It's a culinary repertoire inextricably bound up with our history: from the contributions of the earliest settlers at the Cape and the experimentation with game of stock farmers who trekked into the interior; to the influence of the French, German and British immigrants as well as that of Indian workers and slaves from the East, particularly the Malays, and immigrants from African Countries like Angola and Mozambique. Immigrants from Portugal and Greece have also made their mark.

The first Dutch settlers brought with them recipes and cooking methods that are still with us today; the Dutch habit of serving vegetables dotted with butter and sprinkled with grated nutmeg, for instance. Their way of cooking meat with herbs and spices has also become a time-honoured tradition here.

The chief contribution of the French Huguenots lay in their improvement of viticulture and the production of fruit. They refined the production of raisins, for instance, and their method for making *confitures* from the local fruit survives in the present-day preserves which we call konfyt. The French also passed on their ways of dealing with offal.

The German settlers passed on a love for spicy *wurst*, which we still see today in the wide variety of boerewors recipes, and their hearty casseroles.

British settlers introduced roast meats, particularly beef, which is still the preferred main Sunday meal at many South African tables, served with roast potatoes and Yorkshire pudding. Their savoury pies are legend, as are the filling hot puddings like roly poly, rice pudding and steamed puddings.

Perhaps the greatest contribution was made by the Malay slaves who were brought to the Cape from the East in the late 17th century. We acquired from them the liking for combining sweet and sour that is so characteristic of South African cooking, as well as the spicy sauces, curries, chutneys, blatjangs and atjars that are so indicative of our cuisine.

Many of the old recipes which have become so much a part of South African cooking are included here. There are also recipes that are new classics – if that is not a contradiction in terms – which have become part of our repertoire within the last 40 years or so, but which we have adopted with such alacrity that they feel right at home with those that have been around for centuries.

The recipes have been modernized, in the sense that the present-day utensils and appliances are used – the microwave oven, for instance, where suitable – and that quantities for preserves, pickles and chutneys are smaller to allow for the fact that the modern cook is generally short of time.

Another modernizing feature is that metric measures are provided for all the recipes. One of the problems we encountered when converting and testing the old recipes was the fact that imperial measures and metric ones just do not correspond. We felt, therefore, that giving metric measures would be more useful, as most measuring implements are now metric. If you still prefer to use imperial measures, a table of volume conversions (teaspoon, tablespoon and cup to millilitre/litre) is provided below. Ingredients listed in kilograms and grams in the recipes should be weighed on kitchen scales for the best results.

We hope that you will enjoy using the recipes in this book, and that they will provide pleasure for years to come.

MAGDALEEN VAN WYK AND PAT BARTON

VOLUME EQUIVALENTS

¼ tsp	= 1 ml	¼ cup	= 65 ml
½ tsp	= 2 ml	½ cup	= 125 ml
1 tsp	= 5 ml	¾ cup	= 195 ml
		1 cup	= 250 ml
1 tbsp	= 15 ml	1½ cups	= 375 ml
2 tbsp	= 30 ml	2 cups	= 500 ml
3 tbsp	= 45 ml	3 cups	= 750 ml
4 tbsp	= 60 ml	4 cups	= 1 litre

CHAPTER 1

SOUPS, STARTERS AND SNACKS

Modern hors d'oeuvres or starters did not really feature in the early days of settlement in South Africa. They were introduced, much later, by immigrants from continental Europe. Virtually the only starters or snacks made in those early days were Eastern fish sambals or cooked bone marrow, both served with brown bread and butter. Following the Western European model, soup was then the chosen way to start a meal, and even the humblest kitchen relied on a good soup to stimulate appetites. Spices and flavourings were added during cooking, and the completed dish served at table; cooks considered it an affront to their skill if diners added seasoning to the soup themselves.

STOCK

The constantly simmering stockpot was a prominent feature of every kitchen in days gone by. Into it went every scrap of leftover meat, as well as bones and vegetable trimmings – in fact, virtually everything that could help to improve the flavour of the stock. I remember the old coal range in my grandmother's kitchen, with its big black stockpot (and, of course, the eternal coffee pot!) and I can still taste the delicious ertjiesop (see Green Pea Soup, page 14) and boontjiesop (see Bean Soup, page 14) she used to serve along with her own freshly baked Salt-rising Yeast Bread (page 109), dripping and korrelkonfyt (see Grape Jam, page 130).

The slow cooker is the perfect modern equivalent of the stockpot and can be used for cooking both stocks and soups. For speed and convenience – but only if you are making reasonably small quantities – the microwave oven is ideal.

Stocks are not only a base for soups, although this is their primary use, but they are also used to add flavour to sauces, stews and casseroles.

Stock is perhaps better cooked conventionally on a stove because it needs long, slow cooking for the most flavourful results. If you wish to make stock in your microwave oven, however, do not make more than 2 litres of liquid at a time (depending on the size of your oven). See the individual recipes for microwave times and settings.

HERE ARE SOME TIPS FOR MAKING STOCK:
- Always use a large heavy-based saucepan with a close-fitting lid.
- Soak the bones in cold water for 30 minutes to 1 hour, then heat slowly to boiling point. Use 500 ml to 1 litre water for every 500 g meat and bones.
- For extra flavour and colour, first roast the meat and bones in the oven until browned, or fry them until brown before adding the water.
- Gently simmer the bones and the meat for about 2–3 hours, adding the vegetables, spices, salt and herbs only during the last hour.
- Do not use too many green vegetables when you make stock, as they will impart a bitter flavour.
- Starchy ingredients like potato or thickened gravy will cloud the stock and give it a bitter taste, so add very small quantities or none at all.
- Do not use the water in which bacon or salt beef has been cooked to make stock, as it is far too salty.
- As soon as the stock is cooked, strain it into a clean china or plastic bowl and leave to cool. If the stock is to be used immediately, remove the fat by skimming or mopping the surface of the stock with absorbent kitchen paper. Alternatively, you can leave the stock in the refrigerator, unskimmed, for up to 2 weeks. The fat will harden and will then be easier to remove when the stock is to be used. This layer of fat helps to preserve the stock, as it excludes air.
- Never leave the stock standing in a saucepan – it will become sour.

REHEATING SOUPS IN THE MICROWAVE OVEN:
- Place the soup in a deep, non-metallic container large enough to prevent boiling over.
- Heat, uncovered, until the soup bubbles, stirring several times during heating.
- Heat at 100 per cent power for the following periods: 3 minutes for 250 ml; 6½ minutes for 500 ml; 8½ minutes for 750 ml; and 13 minutes for 1 litre.
- Take particular care when reheating cream- and milk-based soups. They will curdle if they are allowed to boil.

FISH STOCK

1 kg fish heads, bones and trimmings
1 medium onion, sliced
1 medium carrot, sliced
1 stalk celery, chopped
1 bouquet garni (3 sprigs of parsley,
1 sprig of thyme, 1 bay leaf)
1.5 litres water
125 ml dry white wine (optional)
5 ml salt

Rinse the fish bits and pieces very well, then place them in a saucepan with the vegetables, bouquet garni, water and wine. Add the salt and bring slowly to the boil. Remove the scum as it rises to the surface. When there is no scum left, half cover the saucepan and simmer the stock for about 30 minutes. Strain through a fine sieve and cool, then refrigerate or freeze until needed
Makes about 1.25 litres

MICROWAVE OVEN: Place the ingredients in a deep microwave bowl and microwave at 100 per cent power for 8 minutes, or until boiling. Reduce the power to 50 per cent and microwave for 10 minutes.

MEAT (BEEF) STOCK

1 kg shin or neck of beef
30 ml butter or fat
10 ml salt
5 black peppercorns
3 whole cloves
1.5 litres cold water
3 medium carrots, chopped
3 medium turnips, chopped
3 medium leeks, washed well
and chopped
3 stalks celery, chopped
3 medium onions, coarsely chopped
1 bouquet garni (3 sprigs of parsley,
1 sprig of thyme, 1 bay leaf)

Cut the meat from the bone and dice it. Chop the bones into smaller pieces. Melt the butter or fat in a large saucepan and brown the meat and bones. Add the salt, spices and water. Bring to the boil, then cover and simmer for 3–4 hours, skimming the surface when necessary. Add the vegetables and bouquet garni, and simmer for a further hour. Top up with water, then strain through a fine sieve and set aside to cool. Remove the layer of fat that forms on top of the stock and strain it again, if necessary.
Makes about 1 litre

MICROWAVE OVEN: Brown the meat as described in the recipe. Transfer to a large, deep microwave bowl and add the salt, peppercorns, cloves and water. Microwave at 100 per cent power for 8–10 minutes. Add the vegetables and bouquet garni, reduce the power to 50 per cent and microwave for approximately 55 minutes.

GAME STOCK

85 g bacon, diced
1 kg venison, cubed and bones chopped
500 g shin or neck of beef, boned and
meat diced
3.75 litres water
15 ml salt
2 medium carrots, diced
1 large turnip, diced
1 large onion, diced
2 stalks celery, diced
3 white button mushrooms, thinly sliced
6 peppercorns
4 whole cloves
1 bouquet garni (3 sprigs of parsley,
1 sprig of thyme, 1 bay leaf)

Sauté the bacon in a large saucepan over low heat until the fat begins to run. Add the venison, beef and bones, and sauté in the bacon fat until lightly browned. Add the water and gradually bring to the boil. Add the salt and simmer for 1 hour, removing the scum occasionally. Add the vegetables, peppercorns, cloves and bouquet garni, and simmer for a further 3 hours. Strain the stock through a fine sieve. Cool and refrigerate or freeze until needed.
Makes about 2.5 litres

MICROWAVE OVEN: Use 750 g venison and beef, and halve the quantity of water. Sauté the bacon and brown the meat as described in the recipe, then transfer the ingredients to a large microwave dish and microwave at 100 per cent power for 8–10 minutes. Reduce the power to 50 per cent and microwave for about 55 minutes.

CHICKEN STOCK

1.5 kg chicken portions
1 bouquet garni (3 sprigs of parsley,
1 sprig of thyme, 1 bay leaf)
1 clove garlic, crushed
2 whole cloves
6 white peppercorns
10 ml salt
3 litres water
4 medium carrots, sliced
1 medium onion, sliced
3 stalks soup celery, chopped

Place all the ingredients except the vegetables in a large saucepan. Bring to the boil, then simmer, covered, for 1–1½ hours, skimming when necessary. Add the vegetables and continue simmering for 1½–2 hours, or until the chicken is tender. Skim the fat, then strain the stock through a fine sieve. Cool and refrigerate or freeze until needed.
Makes about 2.5 litres

MICROWAVE OVEN: Halve the quantities of chicken, salt, water and celery. Place all the ingredients into a deep microwave bowl and microwave at 100 per cent power for 8–10 minutes. Reduce the power to 50 per cent and microwave for about 55 minutes.
VARIATIONS: Use duck or turkey instead of chicken.

VEGETABLE STOCK

30 ml butter or margarine
30 ml olive oil
6 large carrots, diced
2 large turnips, diced
1 large onion, coarsely chopped
2 large leeks, washed well and coarsely chopped
4 stalks celery, finely chopped
250 ml water
60 g dried beans, soaked overnight in enough water to cover
2 litres water
1 bouquet garni (3 sprigs of parsley, 1 sprig of thyme, 1 bay leaf)
5 ml sugar
10 ml salt
milled black pepper

Melt the butter or margarine in a large saucepan, then add the olive oil. Sauté all the vegetables, except the beans, stirring constantly for about 10–15 minutes, or until they change colour. Add 250 ml water and simmer until the liquid has been absorbed. Add the drained beans and the 2 litres water, mix well and bring to the boil. Skim the fat from the stock, then add the bouquet garni, sugar, salt and pepper. Simmer, covered, for 2–2½ hours. Strain. Cool and refrigerate or freeze until needed.
Makes about 2 litres

WHITE SAUCE

This sauce is used as a base for cream soups.

30 ml butter
30 ml cake four
250 ml milk
salt and milled white pepper

Melt the butter in a heavy-based saucepan over low heat. Remove from the stove. Sprinkle the flour over and stir to blend well. Return to the stove and cook over low heat, stirring, for 2 minutes. Remove from the stove. Gradually add the milk, stirring constantly. Return to the stove, simmer over low heat for 5 minutes and stir often. Season.
Makes 250 ml

MICROWAVE OVEN: Place the butter in a 1 litre glass jug. Microwave at 100 per cent power for 30 seconds, or until melted. Stir in the flour, salt and pepper, and microwave at 100 per cent power for 45 seconds. Stir. Gradually whisk in the milk, blending well. Microwave at 100 per cent power for 2 minutes, stirring twice. Remove from oven and stir well.

VARIATION: For a more intense flavour, make a béchamel sauce. Place 1 carrot, ½ small onion, 1 stalk celery, a pinch of ground mace, 4 peppercorns and the milk in a heavy-based saucepan. Bring to simmering point over low heat, remove from the stove, cover and leave to infuse for 30 minutes. Strain and discard the vegetables. Use instead of milk in the recipe above, or cook in the microwave oven. Microwave the roux at 100 per cent power for 30 seconds. Stir and whisk in the flavoured milk. Microwave at 100 per cent power for 2 minutes, stirring twice.

CREAM OF WATERBLOMMETJIE SOUP

This soup was traditionally served with krakelinge (cracknels) – figure-of-eight-shaped biscuits made from mosbolletjie dough (see Must Buns, page 106), brushed with butter and sprinkled with sugar before baking.

60 ml butter or margarine
2 kg waterblommetjies, trimmed and washed
750 ml Chicken Stock (page 11)
750 ml White Sauce or béchamel sauce (above)
125 ml thick cream
30 ml sherry

Melt the butter or margarine in a heavy-based saucepan over moderate heat. Add the waterblommetjies and toss to coat evenly. Add the stock and simmer, covered, for 20–25 minutes or until the waterblommetjies are soft. Purée the soup and return to the saucepan. Add the sauce and simmer, uncovered, for 10 minutes, stirring constantly. Stir in the cream and sherry, and serve at once.
Serves 4–6

VARIATIONS: This basic recipe can be used to make creamed soups from other green vegetables – celery, broccoli and spinach are particularly good.

CREAM OF CHICKEN SOUP

Stocks add flavour to soups and stews.

The original recipe, as described by Leipoldt and as made by my grandmother and her mother before her, calls for a bunch of mixed herbs, but the traditional bouquet garni does just as well.

15 ml butter or sunflower oil IT
1.5 kg chicken 3lbS
2.5 litres Chicken Stock (page 11) I0c I4c
2 medium onions, sliced
2–3 medium carrots, diced
1 bouquet garni (3 sprigs of parsley or tarragon, 1 sprig of thyme, 1 bay leaf)
250 g cooked rice .55 lbS
15 ml extra butter I T
pinch of ground mace
250 ml coconut milk (see Note) or milk IC
2 egg yolks
250 ml cream IC
freshly grated nutmeg

Melt the butter in a heavy-based saucepan. Add the chicken and brown lightly. Add the stock, onions, carrots and bouquet garni. Simmer, covered, for about 2 hours, or until the chicken is tender. Remove the breast flesh from the chicken and set it aside. Return the rest of the chicken to the saucepan and continue to simmer. Place the breast flesh, the rice, extra butter and mace in a blender or food processor, and chop finely. Add to the saucepan. Simmer for 30 minutes. Add the coconut milk or milk and bring the soup to the boil. Beat the egg yolks and cream together and spoon into a large deep serving dish. Add the soup, grate the nutmeg over and serve immediately.
Serves 6–8

NOTE: To make coconut milk, infuse 125 ml desiccated coconut in 250 ml heated (but not boiled) milk for 1–2 hours. Strain, squeezing the coconut to release all the liquid.

GREEN PEA SOUP (ERTJIESOP)

Green split peas are traditionally used to make this main course soup, but yellow split peas – as used in Holland – also make a delectable dish.

250 ml dried green split peas
1.5 litres water
2 pork shanks or 1 ham bone
4 medium leeks, washed well and
thickly sliced
125 ml finely chopped celery
10 ml salt
milled black pepper
2–4 smoked pork sausages, skinned and
thickly sliced

Soak the peas overnight in the water. Transfer them to a large saucepan, with the water, and add the pork shanks or ham bone. Bring slowly to the boil, then simmer, covered, for about 3 hours, or until the peas are soft and the flavours have combined. Add the leeks, celery, salt and pepper and simmer, covered, for about 30 minutes. Remove the pork shanks or ham bone. Cube the meat, discarding the bones, and return to the soup. Add the sausages and simmer to heat through. Serve immediately, garnished with croutons, grated Cheddar cheese, cream or natural yoghurt and parsley sprigs.
Serves 6

BEAN SOUP (BOONTJIESOP)

The speckled sugar bean was traditionally used to make this nourishing soup. Pork fat (speck) was often used instead of bacon, and a tablespoonful of brown vinegar added to the soup brought out its flavour.

200 g sugar beans
3 mutton or pork shanks, or 1 ham bone
with some meat on it
3 rashers rindless bacon, finely chopped
1.5 litres cold water
30 ml butter or margarine
1 medium onion, finely chopped
2 stalks celery, finely chopped
1 medium carrot, thinly sliced
15 ml salt
2 ml milled pepper

Soak the beans overnight in enough cold water to cover. Drain the beans. Place the meat, bacon and water in a large, heavy-based saucepan. Bring to the boil, then simmer, covered, until the meat is tender (2 hours for mutton or pork shanks, 1 hour for the ham bone). Melt the butter or margarine in a frying pan and sauté the onion, celery and carrot for 3 minutes. When the meat is tender, add the sautéed vegetables and the beans, and simmer, uncovered, for 20–30 minutes. Skim the surface of the soup if necessary. Remove the meat and bones. Cube and reserve the meat and discard the bone, fat and gristle. Purée the remaining contents of the saucepan and return to the saucepan with the meat. Add the salt and pepper and bring the soup to the boil. Serve at once.
Serves 8

VENISON SOUP

Game soup, on which this easier, modern version is based, was usually made from several kinds of venison and game birds, and pork fat (speck) was generally added too. The soup always contained a lot of herbs and spices, and was thickened with flour or bread.

2.5 litres Game Stock (page 11)
4–6 soup bones, with marrow and
some meat
salt and milled pepper
45 ml sherry or dry red wine
1 thick slice brown bread, toasted
and cubed

Place the stock and bones in a large saucepan. Bring to the boil and simmer, covered, for 1–1½ hours, or until the marrow and meat are cooked. Season with salt and pepper, stir in the sherry or wine, and serve poured over toasted brown bread cubes.
Serves 4–6

CURRIED SNOEK HEAD SOUP

This recipe illustrates two points: that nothing edible was ever wasted by our forefathers, and that they were incredibly creative, sometimes combining the most unlikely ingredients to make a delectable dish. Saffron, a favoured spice, not only imparts a reddish yellow colour but also adds pungency to soups. It is expensive, but turmeric makes a good substitute.

4 large snoek heads
30 ml softened butter or sunflower oil
2 large onions, thinly sliced
1 small piece root ginger, crushed
3 cloves garlic, crushed
125 ml thinly sliced celery
2 large potatoes, diced
125 ml cake flour
10 ml salt
1.5 litres water
5 ml turmeric or 2 ml saffron threads
15 ml curry powder
1–2 chillies, seeded and chopped

Wash and halve the snoek heads, retaining the flesh behind the neck. Heat the butter or oil in a large saucepan and sauté the onions for about 5 minutes, or until transparent. Add the ginger, garlic, celery and potatoes. Remove the saucepan from the stove and blend in the flour, stirring to form a smooth paste. Add the salt and water, stirring constantly. Simmer, covered, for 10 minutes. Mix the turmeric or saffron and curry powder to a paste with a little water. Add to the soup, stirring constantly, then stir in the chillies. Add the fish heads and simmer, covered, for about 1½–2 hours, adding more water if necessary. Remove the fish heads and serve the soup at once with brown bread and Moskonfyt (page 127).
Serves 6

Green Pea Soup, Bean Soup and Curried Snoek Head Soup.

TOMATO SOUP

In the past, every household had its own herb garden, where herbs such as basil and thyme were grown. This is a trend which is once again popular, and even flat-dwellers can grow their own selection of herbs in pots on a sunny windowsill. The prawns in this recipe are a modern addition.

500 g ripe tomatoes
25 ml butter or margarine
1 large onion, finely chopped
2 medium potatoes, thinly sliced
10 ml chopped fresh tarragon or basil
1 clove garlic, crushed
250 ml tomato juice
125 ml orange juice
salt and milled pepper
5 ml grated orange rind
250 ml thick cream
250 g cooked prawns, shelled (optional)

Skin and chop the tomatoes. Heat the butter or margarine in a large, heavy-based saucepan and sauté the onions and potatoes for 5–8 minutes, or until the onions are transparent and the potatoes browned.

Add the tomatoes, tarragon or basil, garlic and tomato juice and simmer, covered, for 15 minutes. Purée the soup, return to the saucepan and add the orange juice. Season to taste with salt and pepper and heat through over low heat. Stir in the orange rind, cream and prawns, if using, and serve immediately.

Serves 6

DUMPLING SOUP

This traditional soup was simply a meat broth in which bread dumplings were steamed. In the early days of settlement at the Cape, housewives made the broth from beef, mace, cloves, sorrel, salt and water, but Meat (Beef) Stock (page 11) can be used instead. Reduce the stock slowly and carefully to make sure that its flavour is concentrated enough. The dumplings were made by melting a tablespoon (15 ml) of fat or butter in a cup (250 ml) of boiling water and then blending it with 2 cups (500 ml) of flour. After cooling, 2 eggs were folded in. The dough was shaped into small balls and added to the prepared broth. They were then steamed, covered, for about 15 minutes or until cooked.

SORREL SOUP

As children, we loved to pick sorrel (suring) and chew it for its sour lemon flavour, without knowing how rich it was in vitamin C. Sailors voyaging past the Cape on the Eastern run, a century before Van Riebeeck arrived, knew that it could help prevent scurvy. They landed here to pick the wild sorrel growing on the slopes of Table Mountain and ate it in a stew.

500 g sorrel, washed
1 litre Vegetable Stock (page 12)
1 medium onion, finely chopped
3 medium potatoes, thinly sliced
5 ml chopped fresh thyme
15 ml chopped fresh chives

Soak the sorrel in salted water for 30 minutes. Drain and chop finely. Heat the stock in a large, heavy-based saucepan and add the sorrel, onion and potatoes. Cook, covered, over low heat for approximately 30–45 minutes. Stir in the herbs and serve.

Serves 6

VARIATIONS
- For a creamier result, purée the soup, thicken it with a little flour mixed to a paste with water and stir in milk or cream to taste.
- Finely chopped spinach can be used if preferred or if sorrel is not available.

VEGETABLE SOUP

For a thicker, more substantial winter soup, our ancestors added barley to the vegetables, and included potatoes and swedes or turnips as well.

30 ml sunflower oil
2 medium onions, chopped
1 large clove garlic, crushed
3 large carrots, sliced
2 turnips, sliced
2 stalks celery, chopped
4 baby marrows, sliced
1 small butternut squash, peeled,
seeded and chopped
2 medium brinjals, peeled and diced
kernels cut from 2 fresh mealies
15 ml finely chopped fresh
tarragon or thyme
2 litres Vegetable Stock (page 12) or
Chicken Stock (page 11)
salt and milled pepper

Heat the oil in a large, heavy-based saucepan and sauté the onions and garlic for approximately 5 minutes, or until the onions are transparent. Add the carrots, turnips, celery, baby marrows, butternut squash, brinjals, mealie kernels, tarragon or thyme and the stock and bring the soup to the boil. Reduce the heat, cover the saucepan and simmer for approximately 25 minutes, or until the vegetables are soft. Season to taste and serve.
Serves 4–6

NOTE: Peeled and diced potatoes and tomatoes – about 2 of each – can be added, if you wish.

OXTAIL SOUP

This classic British meat soup, hearty enough to serve as a meal on its own, has become an integral part of the South African culinary heritage. Oxtail needs long, slow cooking, but the results are sublime.

1 oxtail
15 ml butter or dripping
1 large onion, chopped
3 medium carrots, diced
1 medium turnip, thinly sliced
2 medium tomatoes, skinned and
finely chopped
45 ml chopped celery
3 peppercorns
2 whole cloves
2 litres water
1 bouquet garni (3 sprigs of parsley,
1 sprig of thyme, 1 bay leaf)
125 ml cake flour
25 ml sherry or dry red wine (optional)
5 ml salt
1 ml cayenne pepper

Wash the oxtail well and separate it at the joints. Melt the butter or dripping in a heavy-based saucepan. Add the meat and onion, and sauté until the onion is golden and the meat browned. Add the remaining vegetables, peppercorns, cloves, water and bouquet garni, and simmer, covered, for 3 hours. Remove the meat when it is tender and strip it from the bones. Remove the bouquet garni and strain the soup, reserving the stock. Purée the vegetables in a blender or food processor. Add the purée to the stock and return the saucepan to the stove. Mix the flour to a paste with a little water and stir it into the soup to thicken it. Add the sherry or wine, if using, and season with salt and cayenne pepper. Add the meat and serve immediately.
Serves 6

Accompaniments to soup
The early settlers served bits of bread fried in fat, similar to the croutons that are popular today, with rich soups. Soups containing curry sometimes had cooked white rice as an accompaniment, and yet other soups – notably those originating in the East – were served with Bokkems (page 26), or Indian duck as it was called by the British colonials who came to the country from India and Malaysia.

SMOKED SNOEK PÂTÉ

This is a less spicy version of the popular fish sambal introduced to this country from the East, which our forefathers savoured (see Snoek Sambal, page 19).

125 g butter or margarine, softened
wholegrain mustard to taste
prepared English mustard to taste
65 ml brandy
250 g smoked snoek, boned and flaked
salt and milled pepper

Beat the butter or margarine in a mixing bowl until creamy. Add the mustards and beat to mix well. Add the brandy and beat well. Add the flaked snoek and mix well to combine thoroughly. Season and pack into earthenware jars. Chill until firm. Serve with biscuits, Melba toast or wholewheat bread. The pâté will keep for about 1 week, refrigerated.
Serves 4

NOTE: it is very easy to make larger quantities of this pâté if you are feeding a crowd; simply ensure that the quantity of snoek is double that of the butter or margarine. Adjust the quantity of brandy to taste.

Snoek Sambal and Smoked Snoek Pâté, delicious with bread or Melba toast.

SPRINGBOK LIVER PÂTÉ

The abundance of game and the unpalatability of the beef available in the 17th and 18th centuries meant that many game dishes made their way into our culinary repertoire. This game pâté occupies a well-deserved place among the many meat- and fish-based pâtés that have become firm favourites as the start to a meal.

30 ml butter
500 g springbok liver, skinned and sliced
250 g brown mushrooms, finely chopped
1 small onion, finely chopped
125 ml dry sherry or dry white wine
1 clove garlic, crushed
1 ml dill seeds
5 ml salt
4 drops Tabasco® sauce
175 g butter
1 bay or lemon leaf

Melt the 30 ml butter in a frying pan, then add the liver, mushrooms and onion, and sauté for 5 minutes. Stir in the sherry or wine, garlic, dill seeds, salt and Tabasco® sauce and simmer, covered, for 5–8 minutes, or until the liver is just tender. Remove from the stove and allow to cool slightly. Place in a blender or food processor with the 175 g butter and purée until smooth. Pack the pâté tightly into an earthenware dish or jar, and garnish with the bay or lemon leaf. Chill for at least 6 hours before use, to allow flavours to mingle (see Note). Serve with Melba toast, wholewheat bread or savoury biscuits.

Serves 6–8

NOTE: The pâté improves if left to mature for a day or two, but it has a limited shelf life – up to 5 days in the refrigerator. If making it in advance, spoon clarified butter over the top to help preserve it.

SNOEK SAMBAL

The recipe for fish sambals – very spicy fish spreads – was brought to this country by Malay slaves at the end of the 17th century and quickly adapted for the fish available locally. Cooked, flaked snoek – some cooks prefer to use dried salted snoek (see page 30) – is one of the best fish for this snack, which was traditionally served with moskonfyt.

500 g cooked snoek, boned and flaked
1 medium onion, finally chopped
2 ml chilli or Tabasco® sauce
10 ml vinegar
2 ml salt
2 ml milled pepper
5–10ml Moskonfyt (page 127)

Mix all the ingredients together well and pack the mixture into an earthenware dish. Serve with thinly sliced brown bread and butter. The sambal will keep for 2 days in the refrigerator.

Serves 4

CRUMBED ANCHOVIES

In the past, anchovies were plentiful and were often braaied on the beach. Fresh anchovies are not as freely available today, but frozen fish may also be used.

400 g fresh or frozen anchovies
50 ml cake flour
1 egg
15 ml milk
125 ml dried breadcrumbs
sunflower oil
coarse salt

Dust the anchovies with flour. Beat the egg and milk together and dip the fish in the mixture. Roll the fish in the breadcrumbs, coating them completely. Deep-fry in hot oil, then drain on absorbent paper. Sprinkle the fish with coarse salt and serve them immediately as part of an antipasto tray or with drinks.

Serves 8

VARIATION: Use sardines instead of the anchovies.

MILK NOODLES (MELKKOS, MELKSNYSELS)

Milk noodles were traditionally served as a light supper dish.

Melkkos was served as a light supper dish, in the days when the main meal was served in the middle of the day. It makes an interesting first course to a traditional meal. To save time, ready-made medium ribbon noodles, vermicelli or thin ribbon noodles can be used, but the dish tastes much better if you make the noodles yourself as described here.

500 ml bread flour
5 ml salt
2 eggs
1.5 litres milk
30 ml butter
Cinnamon Sugar (page 21)

Sift the flour and salt together. Beat the eggs well, then add 250 ml of the milk and mix well. Stir in the sifted flour mixture and just enough milk to form a stiff dough. Knead until elastic, then roll the dough out thinly on a floured board. Sprinkle the dough with additional flour and cut into 3 mm-wide strips to make noodles. Heat the remaining milk to boiling point. Add the noodles and butter, and simmer for about 30 minutes, or until the noodles are cooked. Ladle the melkkos into soup bowls and serve hot, sprinkled with Cinnamon Sugar.
Serves 6

RAREBIT

Welsh rarebit, a tangy cheese mixture, is spread onto toast and grilled to make a perfect starter or quick snack. It was introduced to South Africa by the British.

30 ml butter or margarine
60 ml cake flour
125 ml milk
500 ml grated mature Cheddar cheese
5 ml prepared mustard of your choice
10 ml Worcestershire sauce
salt and milled pepper
4 slices toast

Melt the butter or margarine in a small saucepan over low heat. Add the flour and cook for about 2–3 minutes, stirring. Gradually add the milk, stirring constantly for about 3 minutes, or until the mixture is smooth and thick. Add most of the cheese, the mustard, Worcestershire sauce, salt and pepper, and stir until the cheese has melted. Spread on the toast, sprinkle the remaining cheese on top and grill until the cheese is bubbling and golden. Serve at once.
Serves 4

VARIATION: To make a more substantial snack, top the rarebit with a poached or fried egg.

CHILLI BITES (DHALTJIES)

These hot, fiery snacks, which are very popular among the Malay and Indian communities, are definitely not for the faint-hearted!

250 ml pea flour
30 ml cake flour
1 small onion, finely grated
5 ml ground cumin
5 ml ground coriander
10 ml crushed dried chillies
5 ml salt
3 ml turmeric
½ bunch fresh coriander
leaves, chopped
1 small tart green apple, cored
and grated
few spinach leaves, shredded
water
5 ml baking powder
500 ml sunflower oil

Sift the pea flour and cake flour into a large mixing bowl. Add the onion, cumin, coriander, chillies, salt, turmeric, coriander leaves, apple and spinach, and mix with just enough water to make a stiff batter. Set aside until ready to make the chilli bites, then stir in the baking powder. Heat the oil in a deep saucepan. Drop tablespoonfuls of the mixture into the oil, a few at a time, and deep-fry for about 5 minutes, or until lightly browned. Turn the chilli bites to brown the other side if necessary, then remove and drain on absorbent paper. Repeat until the mixture has all been used. Serve hot.

Makes about 24

CINNAMON SUGAR

Ground cinnamon mixed with sugar has always been a favourite flavouring or finish for dishes like melktert (see Milk Tart, page 101), Pumpkin Fritters (page 71) and Traditional Pancakes (page 89). To make, add about 5 ml ground cinnamon to every 65 ml granulated sugar and mix well.

SNOEK ROE PÂTÉ

Snoek roe has always been considered a delicacy among the fisherfolk of the West Coast. One of the best ways to enjoy it is fried (preferably on the beach), but this elegant pâté is an excellent alternative.

250 g snoek roe
juice of 1 lemon
150 ml thick cream or 75 g butter,
softened and made up to 150 ml
with milk
pinch of ground ginger
pinch of cayenne pepper
pinch of paprika

Remove and discard the skins from the roe, then empty the eggs into a bowl. Add half the lemon juice and mix it in well with a fork, taking care not to break the eggs (see Note). Add remaining lemon juice and mix again. Gradually mix in the cream. Season to taste with ginger and cayenne pepper. Transfer the pâté to a serving dish, sprinkle with paprika and refrigerate until ready to serve. Serve with hot buttered toast. It will keep for 2 days in the refrigerator.

Serves 4

NOTE: Do not use an electric mixer or blender, which would break the eggs (roe).

CHAPTER 2

FISH AND SEAFOOD

In the past, our seas teemed with all kinds of fish and seafood. In coastal towns, from the shores of Namibia right round to Mozambique, inhabitants enjoyed the bounty of the sea. Until a few decades ago, the people of Cape Town could buy fish directly from fishing boats, which landed at a sandy cove at the bottom of Adderley Street, and the tradition continued at Kalk Bay and Hout Bay on the Atlantic seaboard throughout most of the last century. Sadly, this is now a mere memory for most of us, although Kalk Bay still offers fresh fish for sale from the boats, and now and then you can still see hawkers selling fish from horse-drawn carts or hear the mournful cry of the fish horn, once so common. There is one other exception – KwaZulu-Natal, where the annual sardine run not only provides plenty of fun, but also a rich harvest of these tasty little fish.

BRAISED SNOEK (SMOORSNOEK) *Mackerel*

Braising was one of the most popular cooking methods in the early days of settlement in the Cape, partly because of the utensils that were available and partly because it was the ideal way to combine the flavours of the ingredients. Smoorsnoek was, and still is, a popular dish among the Malay inhabitants of our country. Although using snoek is traditional, the Malays also use other fish and the dish is then called smoorvis (braised fish). The green pepper is a Western substitute for the fiery green chilli they generally use.

30 ml sunflower oil
15 ml butter or margarine
1 large onion, chopped
2 cloves garlic, crushed
2 large potatoes, thinly sliced
2 medium tomatoes, skinned and quartered
1 small green sweet pepper, seeded and chopped
1 kg cooked fresh snoek or smoked snoek, boned and flaked

5 ml salt
2 ml milled pepper

Heat the oil and butter or margarine in a saucepan and sauté the onion and garlic for about 5 minutes, or until the onion is transparent. Add the potatoes and sauté for about 5 minutes, or until starting to soften, stirring often. Add the tomatoes, green pepper and flaked snoek. Shake the saucepan to mix the ingredients well and simmer for 10–15 minutes, or until the fish is heated through. Add the salt and pepper and mix well. Serve with cooked rice and a green salad, garnish with sliced lemon.
Serves 6

Snoek in a barrel
Not so very long ago, it was the custom to 'cure' snoek in order to preserve it. The snoek was cut into pieces and placed in a brine solution to which saltpetre and lemon leaves were added, and then it was stored in a large wooden barrel. It was left to mature for approximately a week before using; each time the housewife needed a piece of fish, she removed it from the brine solution, rinsed it off and either baked it or used it in a bredie or stew. This method of preserving snoek probably comes from the Dutch way of preserving herring in brine. Meat was also preserved in this way.

Braised Snoek and Snoek Curry, two appetising ways to serve this kind of fish.

SNOEK CURRY

Perhaps the best-known and most versatile Cape fish is the snoek. The Malays discovered long ago that serving it in a curry sauce was a dish fit for the gods.

I kg unsalted snoek, sliced
5 ml salt
2 ml milled pepper
juice of ½ lemon
sunflower oil
I large onion, finely chopped
2 cloves garlic, crushed
15 ml curry powder
5 ml turmeric
10 ml cake flour
250 ml water
2 allspice berries
I bay or lemon leaf
5 ml vinegar
20 ml sugar
15 ml smooth apricot jam

Season the snoek with salt and pepper, sprinkle with the lemon juice and set aside. Heat a little oil in a saucepan and sauté the onion and garlic for about 5 minutes, or until the onion is transparent. Add the curry powder and the turmeric, and mix well. Sprinkle the flour over and stir it in. Add the water and bring to the boil, stirring. Reduce the heat to low and add the snoek, allspice and bay or lemon leaf. Simmer, covered, for 15 minutes. Mix the vinegar, sugar and apricot jam, and add to the saucepan. Simmer, stirring occasionally, for another 15 minutes. Add more salt and pepper if necessary. Serve immediately with cooked rice or crushed wheat.
Serves 6

VARIATIONS: Other firm-fleshed fish can be used instead of snoek, for example, yellowtail.

BRAAIED WHOLE SNOEK

My childhood memories are peppered with recollections of family visits to the beach at Bloubergstrand. The most important part of this well-planned occasion was buying the fresh snoek from the hawkers' carts along the way, and then braaiing the fish on the beach. Later memories are of freshly caught galjoen on the Namibian coast at Henties Bay – different location, same tradition.

I whole fresh snoek, entrails removed
30 ml melted butter or margarine
15 ml salt
5 ml milled pepper
15 ml fresh lemon juice

Wash the snoek well and pat it dry. Brush with melted butter or margarine. Season, inside and out, with salt and pepper and sprinkle a little lemon juice in the cavity. Open the snoek out flat and place, skin-side down, on the braai grid (a hinged grid is best). Braai the snoek low over hot coals for 3 minutes on each side, then raise the grid to 30 cm above the coals and braai for a further 15 minutes on each side. Baste the snoek often with melted butter. Serve with Baked Sweet Potatoes (page 75), or wholewheat bread and Grape Jam (page 130).
Serves 8–10

VARIATIONS: Other large fish can also be braaied in this way – galjoen, for instance – or whole smaller fish like harders, red roman and elf (shad)

FISH IN BANANA LEAVES

On the tropical coast of Natal, fish has been cooked in banana leaves for generations, in much the same way as fish is cooked in dampened newspaper. The fish is cleaned and gutted, seasoned inside and out, and brushed with melted butter, then wrapped well in clean banana leaves and places on a bed of embers. Some of the embers are piled on top of the parcel and it is left to cook slowly. Alternatively, the parcel can be steamed in a large fish kettle over the coals, making the dish a kind of potjiekos.

HARDERS OVER THE COALS

Harders (mullet) braaied over the coals are traditionally served with Baked Sweet Potatoes (page 75). These flavourful little fish have long formed part of the staple diet of fishermen along our coast. Cooked over the coals, fried, used in stews or dried to make Bokkems (below), they are a vital source of nutrition.

125 ml sunflower oil
2 cloves garlic, crushed
6 fresh harders, cleaned and gutted
salt and milled pepper

Heat the oil lightly in a small, cast-iron frying pan over the coals, add the garlic and sauté for about 5 minutes, or until the garlic is transparent. Remove the pan from the coals and set it aside for about 10 minutes to allow the flavours to mingle. Remove the garlic with a slotted spoon and discard it. Brush the harders with the oil, inside and out. Season the fish with salt and milled pepper, and braai over moderate coals for about 10 minutes on each side, or until cooked through. Serve immediately.
Serves 6

BOKKEMS

Bokkems are salted, dried harders, once a staple food along the West Coast where they were eaten like Biltong (page 53) or soaked in fresh water to remove excess salt and then added to stews.

harders
coarse cooking salt

Gut the harders (it is not necessary to scale them) and wash them thoroughly. Salt the fish very well and layer them in a large container. Leave the container in a cool place overnight. Next day, remove the fish from the salt and thread a length of strong twine through the heads to form bunches of 10–20 fish. Hang the fish out in a windy place until dry – a few days – but bring them in overnight.

VARIATION: Snoek may be salted and dried in the same way, but the fish must first be 'vlekked' – opened along the backbone without cutting it in two. To use, soak the snoek in water to remove most of the salt, then use in recipes like smoorsnoek (see Braised Snoek, page 24).

FISH BOBOTIE

This aromatic version of the traditional meat bobotie was once common fare in the coastal areas, as fish was cheap and freely available.

500 g cooked white fish, skinned and boned
1 thick slice crustless white bread
300 ml milk
65 ml butter or margarine
1 large onion, coarsely chopped
juice of 1 lemon
10 ml curry powder
30 ml seedless raisins
30 ml chopped blanched almonds
5 ml salt
1 ml milled pepper
2 large eggs
2 bay or lemon leaves

Flake the fish and place in a bowl. Soak the bread in the milk. Melt the butter or margarine and sauté the onion for 5 minutes, or until transparent. Add the lemon juice, curry powder, raisins, almonds, salt and pepper, and cook for 1 minute. Add the fish. Squeeze the milk from the bread and reserve it. Add the bread to the fish mixture and combine well. Beat the eggs, add the reserved milk and blend well. Pour the fish mixture into a greased ovenproof dish. Pour the egg mixture over the top with the bay or lemon leaves. Bake at 190 °C for 35 minutes, or until set. Serve with rice and bowls of desiccated coconut, Fruit Chutney (page 136) and sambals (see recipes on pages 76 and 77) of your choice.
Serves 6

PICKLED FISH (INGELEGDE VIS)

One of the best-known Cape dishes, pickled fish was perfected by the Malays who served it at funeral feasts. This fish curry is eaten cold. In the past, ingelegde vis was also packed in jars with a layer of fat on top to keep the air out, so enabling it to be stored for many months.

2 kg Cape salmon, kingklip, yellowtail or
any other firm-fleshed white fish
4 large onions, sliced
750 ml vinegar
125 ml water
20 ml salt
125 ml sugar
40 ml curry powder
15 ml turmeric
2 ml cayenne pepper
1 piece root ginger, crushed
10 coriander seeds
5 lemon or bay leaves

Clean and fillet the fish and cut it into portions. Combine all the other ingredients in a deep saucepan and simmer for 20 minutes. Add the fish and simmer for a further 20 minutes, taking care not to break the fish. Remove with a slotted spoon and layer into a glass dish. Pour the curry sauce over. Leave to cool, then cover tightly and leave to mature in the refrigerator for at least 3 days before use, but preferably longer. Serve with brown bread and butter.

Serves 8–10

FISH POTJIE

Potjiekos – cooking food in a three-legged cast-iron pot suspended over the coals – has been a South African tradition since the days when travellers ventured into the unexplored interior of the country. Game was plentiful when the Voortrekkers and the transport riders travelled the country in their ox wagons, and venison was extensively used. Because of the current popularity of this cooking method, however, all kinds of food are now used to make potjiekos. Seafood makes a delectable potjie, but this combination of white fish and seafood is much more economical and just as tasty.

10 ml sunflower oil
1 medium onion, sliced
2 cloves garlic, crushed
1 medium green sweet pepper, seeded
and sliced or 1 green chilli, seeded
and chopped
2 tuna steaks, trimmed
500 g hake or kingklip, filleted and cut
into portions
24–36 mussels, cleaned
5 ml salt
5 ml chopped fresh oregano
1 bay leaf
5 ml lemon juice
30 ml tomato paste
125 ml beer or dry white wine

Heat the oil in a cast-iron pot and sauté the onion and garlic for about 5 minutes, or until the onion is transparent. Add the green pepper or chilli, tuna, hake or kingklip and mussels, then stir in the remaining ingredients. Simmer over the coals for 30–45 minutes, or until the fish is tender. Serve immediately with Pot Bread (page 109) or cooked brown rice.

Serves 6

BRAISED PERLEMOEN

Perlemoen or abalone is considered a great delicacy. The shells are a familiar sight in many a South African home, where they serve as ashtrays or mementoes of a seaside holiday.

6–8 perlemoen
30 ml butter or margarine
125 ml dry white wine
50 ml dried breadcrumbs
1 ml freshly grated nutmeg
salt and milled pepper

Remove the perlemoen from their shells with a sharp, strong knife. Trim the flesh, then scrub the flat dark side vigorously with a hard brush or pot scourer. Cut into steaks and beat well with a mallet. (It is important to clean and pound them really well, or they will be tough when cooked.) Simmer the steaks in a little water in a saucepan, covered, for 45 minutes, or until tender when tested with a skewer. (They can also be steamed with a little water in a pressure cooker for 30 minutes.) Dice or mince and sauté in the butter or margarine in a saucepan until browned. Add the wine, breadcrumbs and nutmeg, and season well. Simmer, uncovered, for 5 minutes. Serve on rice, with lemon wedges. **Serves 6–8**

CURRIED ALIKREUKEL FRIKKADELS

Alikreukel (periwinkles) are seldom available commercially, but are still found along our rocky coastline. This recipe perfectly illustrates the marriage between Dutch and Eastern culinary traditions: frikkadels by the Dutch settlers and spicy curry sauces by the Indians and Malays.

24 alikreukel
1 large onion, chopped
1 clove garlic, crushed
10 ml curry powder
2 slices crustless white bread soaked in
50 ml milk
1 large egg, beaten
30 ml finely chopped fresh parsely
5 ml salt
5 ml lemon juice
cake flour
sunflower oil

Place the alikreukel in a saucepan, cover with cold water and boil in the shell for about 20 minutes. Remove the flesh from the shell with a long pin. Cut off the flat disk from one end and the intestines from the other. Wash the arikeukel very well under cold running water to remove all the sand, then mince the flesh. Mix the minced alikreukel with all the other ingredients, except the flour and oil, and shape into small frikkadels. Dust with a little flour. Fry the frikkadels in heated oil for about 5 minutes on either side, or until lightly browned and cooked through. Drain the frikkadels on absorbent paper and serve hot with stir-fried vegetables or cooked rice. **Serves 6**

PRAWNS PERI-PERI

This recipe was brought to South Africa by Portuguese settlers – mostly from Mozambique and Angola – and has become a favourite among South Africans. It is a quicker version of the original, in which the prawns were marinated in olive oil, lemon juice, garlic, bay leaves, peri-peri powder and ground cloves before cooking.

50 ml butter
36–42 prawns, heads and veins removed

PERI-PERI SAUCE
200 g butter
2 ml Tabasco® sauce

Melt the 50 ml butter in a large frying pan and stir-fry the prawns for 5 minutes, or until they turn ink. To make the sauce, combine the 200 g butter with the Tabasco® sauce and heat until the butter melts. Serve the prawns on a bed of cooked rice, topped with the peri-peri sauce. **Serves 6**

NOTE: The Portuguese make a piquant peri-peri sauce, which is used sparingly for seasoning, by half filling a small bottle with olive oil and immersing the scraped-off upper part of small red chillies in it. The oil is allowed to mature for a few months before using. A little of this can be used instead of the Tabasco® sauce in the recipe above.

CURRIED CRAYFISH

The Malays traditionally served crayfish curried.

Crayfish is no longer as plentiful as in the days when it was a regular item on the menu of fisherman all around our coastline. They enjoyed it simply boiled, and purists still say that this is the best way to savour the sweetness of its delicate flesh. This traditional Malay recipe for curried crayfish, however, is an aromatic blend of flavours that will have even the purists salivating.

4 cooked crayfish
75 ml butter or margarine
1 large onion, coarsely chopped
1 small clove garlic, crushed
15 ml curry powder
15 ml cake flour
2 medium ripe tomatoes,
  seeded and skinned
1 medium tart green apple,
  cored and grated
15 ml smooth apricot jam
250 ml Fish Stock (page 10)
50 ml dry white wine
2 ml lemon juice

Carefully remove all the crayfish flesh from the shells and chop it coarsely. Set the flesh aside and reserve the tail shells. Melt the butter or margarine in a large saucepan and sauté the onion and garlic for about 5 minutes, or until transparent. Add the curry powder, stirring well. Remove the saucepan from the stove, add the flour and stir it in well to make a smooth paste. Return the saucepan to the stove. Add the tomatoes, apple, jam, stock, wine and lemon juice, and simmer, covered, for 15 minutes. Stir in the reserved crayfish flesh and heat the mixture through. Spoon the hot crayfish mixture into the tail shells and serve the curry with cooked rice and fresh pineapple, banana and pawpaw as side dishes.
Serves 4

STEAMED BLACK MUSSELS

12 mussels per person

Soak the mussels in cold water for 1½ hours, discarding those that float on the surface or that open. Using a small knife, scrape off the beards, then scrub the mussels under cold running water to remove all the sand and grit. Place the mussels in a wire basket suspended over boiling water in a saucepan, taking care not to let the water touch the mussels. Steam, covered, for about 10 minutes, or until the shells open. Discard any mussels that haven't opened. Serve immediately with garlic butter sauce or lemon butter sauce (see Note).

NOTE: To make garlic (or lemon) butter sauce, melt 100 g butter over low heat, add 2 crushed cloves of garlic (or 5 ml lemon juice) and 2 ml salt, and shake or stir well. Serve immediately.

Dried fish
The south-western coast of the Cape is the world of salted and dried fish. If you drive along the coastal road from Cape Town towards Lamberts Bay, you will see gevlekte (butterflied) whole snoek and bokkems hanging out to dry on stands erected alongside sun-washed, windswept bays.

Steamed Black Mussels, a favourite treat of holiday-makers along our coastline.

OYSTERS ON THE SHELL

Oysters occur naturally along the south and east coast of the Cape, but recently a cultivated oyster industry was set up at Knysna. The best way to enjoy oysters, say most lovers of this seafood delicacy, is to eat them untainted by any stewing, mincing, frying or other frills. Serve the oysters on the half shell, well chilled, nestling on a bed of crushed ice, with lemon juice or Tabasco® sauce, if desired.

KEDGEREE

The kedgeree served at 18th and 19th century tables in the Cape was vastly different from the present-day one made with steamed haddock, even though they have the same origins. The dish probably came from Batavia, brought here by the Dutch. British colonials from India brought another version with them, which is probably the basis of the modern dish.

250 ml uncooked rice
375 ml cooked, boned and chopped fish
or crayfish
2 small hard-boiled eggs, chopped
butter or margarine
1 small onion, cut into rings
1 small red chilli, seeded and chopped
salt and milled pepper
freshly grated nutmeg
10 ml butter

Boil the rice in salted water for 20 minutes, or until tender. Drain and steam it over simmering water while preparing the fish or crayfish. Mix the fish or crayfish with the eggs and set aside. Heat a little butter or margarine in a frying pan and sauté the onion and chilli for 5 minutes. Add salt, pepper and nutmeg to taste, and stir to mix. Add 10 ml butter and, when melted, add the rice and the fish or crayfish mixture and stir. Simmer for 15 minutes, or until well combined and heated through, shaking the pan from time to time to prevent sticking and burning.
Serves 4–6

SMOKED SNOEK

The old-fashioned home method of smoking any kind of fish took place in a specially constructed smokehouse or, more informally, over untreated wood shavings in a large drum. The modern method, which is actually smoke roasting, is less time-consuming but the results are every bit as delicious.

1.5 kg snoek portions
salt
untreated oak wood shavings

Season the fleshy side of the snoek portions very well with salt, then chill for 1 hour, or until firm. Sprinkle the wood shavings in the base of a heavy-based saucepan with a tight-fitting lid. Place the fish in a metal container (an aluminium foil dish is easiest) and stand it on a trivet or pot stand in the saucepan. Close the saucepan tightly with the lid and smoke the snoek for approximately 15 minutes on high, then about 10–20 minutes on low, depending on the size and thickness of the fish.
Serves 4–6

VARIATIONS: Whole trout, salmon trout or angelfish portions can also be smoked in this way.

FISH CAKES

This is another traditional way to use up leftover cooked fish, which can be served with a spicy tomato or curry sauce for a delicious family meal.

750 g cooked white fish, boned
1 large onion, chopped and parboiled
30 ml chopped fresh parsley or
1 small green chilli, seeded and
finely chopped
1 slice crustless white bread, soaked in
a little milk
1 large egg, beaten
salt and milled pepper
cake flour
sunflower oil

Mince the fish, onion, parsley or chilli and soaked bread together. Add the egg, salt and pepper to taste and shape the mixture into patties about 2 cm thick. Dust with cake flour. Heat the oil in a large frying pan and fry the fish cakes for approximately 5 minutes on either side, or until they are browned. Drain them on absorbent paper and serve with lemon wedges or a spicy sauce and cooked rice.
Serves 4

CHAPTER 3

POULTRY

There were plenty of game birds distributed throughout the African subcontinent when Van Riebeeck arrived, but chickens were introduced from Europe, as were domestic ducks and later, turkeys. It was the custom not to slaughter chickens until their laying days were over, so the meat had to have special treatment to make it tender and succulent. Long, slow cooking was the order of the day: potroasts, braised dishes, stews and – once the Malays and Indians had introduced them – curries.

ROAST STUFFED CHICKEN

Roast Stuffed Chicken, served with roast potatoes, green beans and patty pans.

Seventy or so years ago, chicken, especially roast chicken, held pride of place as the main meal of the week: it was usually served on Sunday for lunch or dinner. The chickens were all free-range, which meant that the white breast meat, as well as the dark meat of the thighs and legs, was much more flavourful.

1.5–2 kg chicken, cleaned and trimmed
Sage and Onion Stuffing (page 35)
salt and milled pepper
30–45 ml margarine, butter,
**   chicken fat or sunflower oil**

Fill the chicken with the stuffing and close the openings with a skewer or thread. Truss the chicken, if desired, and place it on a grid, uncovered, in a deep roasting pan. Season with the salt and pepper, and rub the margarine, butter, chicken fat or oil all over the bird. Cover the bottom of the roasting pan with water. Roast at 200 °C for 30 minutes. Lower the temperature to 180 °C and continue roasting, basting occasionally, for another 45 minutes to 1 hour. Cover the roasting pan with foil if the chicken browns too much. Serve it with Giblet Gravy (page 36), roast potatoes and steamed vegetables.
Serves 4–6

VARIATIONS
- Fill a 4.5 kg turkey with a double quantity of Forcemeat Stuffing (page 35) and proceed as in the recipe above, roasting for a total of 3–3½ hours at the same temperatures.
- Fill a 2 kg duck with Orange and Raisin Stuffing (page 35) and proceed as above, roasting for a total of 2 hours at the same temperatures.

Stuffings and farces
Nowadays most stuffings are based on herbs, onions and breadcrumbs, but the early colonists made use of what was available, for example dried apricots, peaches and prunes, or vegetables like green mealies. They also gathered wild edible mushrooms to use in stuffings.

FORCEMEAT STUFFING

This stuffing is traditionally used for turkey, but it is excellent with chicken as well.

500 g pork or beef sausage meat
100 g streaky bacon, shredded
125 ml fresh white breadcrumbs
15 ml chopped fresh parsley
1 large egg

pinch of dried mixed herbs
salt and milled pepper

Mix all the ingredients well in a bowl.
Makes enough for a 1.5 kg chicken

SAGE AND ONION STUFFING

Shredded suet or beef fat and egg are the binding agents in this traditional stuffing for chicken or lamb.

500 ml fresh white breadcrumbs
60 g prepared shredded suet
5 ml salt
2 ml milled pepper
1 medium onion, finely chopped
15 ml finely chopped fresh sage
1 large egg
15 ml milk

Mix the breadcrumbs, suet, salt and pepper. Blanch the onion in boiling water for 2–3 minutes, then drain well and stir into the breadcrumb mixture. Stir in the sage. Beat the egg and milk together, add to the dry ingredients and mix well.
Makes enough to stuff a 1.5–2 kg chicken or 2 kg leg of lamb

ORANGE AND RAISIN STUFFING

The flavour of oranges goes particularly well with duck and also helps to tenderize the flesh of game birds like Muscovy duck (see Pot-roast Muscovy Duck, page 64).

500 g fresh white breadcrumbs
2 ml each salt and milled pepper
finely grated rind of 1 small lemon
juice and finely grated rind of 1 small orange
25 ml cubed butter or margarine
100 ml seedless raisins
20 ml finely chopped fresh parsley
1 large egg, beaten

Combine the breadcrumbs, salt, pepper, lemon and orange rind. Rub in the butter or margarine until crumbly, then stir in the raisins and parsley. Add the orange juice and egg and mix well to bind.
Makes enough for a 2 kg duck or Muscovy duck

ALMOND STUFFING

The Dutch brought recipes for sweet and savoury stuffings to the Cape with them. Almond stuffing was used for poultry.

3 large eggs, separated
250 ml thick cream
pinch of freshly grated nutmeg
100 g ground almonds
180 g dried breadcrumbs
60 ml diced butter

Mix the egg yolks with the cream and nutmeg until well combined. Mix the ground almonds with a little of the egg white and stir the mixture into the egg yolk mixture. Stir in the breadcrumbs and diced butter. Add the stiffly beaten egg whites. Beat the mixture until smooth and fairly stiff.
Makes enough for a 1.5–2 kg chicken

GIBLET GRAVY

chicken giblets
salted water
dripping from roast
60 ml cake flour
15 ml chopped fresh parsley
5 ml salt
2 ml milled pepper

Boil the neck, gizzard and heart in salted water until tender, about 2 hours. Add the liver and boil for a further 15 minutes. Drain off the stock and make it up to 500 ml with water. Dice the meat, discarding the gristle and bone. Heat the dripping in a saucepan, stir in the flour and cook until foamy. Gradually stir in the stock and cook, stirring, for about 3 minutes, or until the gravy thickens. Stir in the diced giblets and parsley, season with salt and pepper and serve.
Makes about 500 ml

BREAD SAUCE

This classic sauce was introduced by the British, who served it primarily with Roast Beef (page 42). It also makes an aromatic accompaniment to chicken.

1 medium onion
4 whole cloves
100 ml milk
250 ml fresh white breadcrumbs
salt and milled pepper
pinch of ground mace
30 ml butter
15 ml cream

Peel the onion and stud with cloves. Place it in a saucepan with the milk and bring slowly to the boil. Place the breadcrumbs in a small dish and pour the milk over. Add the onion. Season with the salt, pepper and mace, then stir in the butter and cream. Place in the coolest part of the oven while roasting the meat and leave for 15 minutes. Remove the onion and serve.

VARIATION: Place the breadcrumbs in a small saucepan with the onion and cloves, and add the milk. Simmer very slowly over low heat for 15 minutes, then add the remaining ingredients.

OLD-FASHIONED CHICKEN PIES

These pies, with their delectable pastry, held centre stage as part of the Christmas celebrations in the 17th and 18th centuries. Quick Flaky Pastry (page 100) is very quick to use, and the result is delicious.

250 g Quick Flaky Pastry (page 100) or
Puff Pastry (page 100)
2 hard-boiled eggs, shelled and sliced
1 egg yolk mixed with a little milk

FILLING
2 kg chicken, cut into portions
6 allspice berries
6 peppercorns
3 whole cloves
6 blades mace
2 medium onions, sliced
10 ml salt
200 ml Chicken Stock (page 11)
30 ml sago
150 ml dry white wine
1 egg yolk
10 ml lemon juice

First make the filling. Stew the chicken pieces with the allspice berries, peppercorns, cloves, mace, onions, salt and stock until tender. Remove the spices and bones, and cut the meat into smaller pieces. Soak the sago in water until soft and add to the chicken. Add the wine and simmer until the sago is transparent. Stir in the egg yolk and lemon juice. Remove from the stove and cool slightly. Roll out the pastry and use to line 6 small pie dishes. Spoon in the chicken filling and place a few slices of hard-boiled egg on top. Cover with the remaining flaky pastry, crimping the pastry edges together. Make slits in the top of the pastry, brush with the egg yolk mixture and bake the pies at 200 °C for 15–20 minutes, or until golden. Serve with Yellow Rice with Raisins (page 72) and chutney of your choice.
Serves 6

VARIATION: Bake 1 large chicken pie instead of 6 small ones. (The pies can also be served cold.)

BRAISED DUCK WITH DRIED FRUIT

The combination of savoury and sweet flavours in one dish is peculiarly South African, and the idea was probably a legacy of the Malay cooks whom the Dutch at the Cape employed because of their flair for food, of which this recipe is a good example.

1.75–2 kg duck
10 ml salt
2 ml white pepper
5 ml chopped fresh mixed herbs
50 ml sunflower oil
150 ml apple juice
100 ml Chicken Stock (page 11)
250 g mixed dried fruit, soaked in water until plump
10 ml cake flour or cornflour
20 ml cold water

Wipe and trim the duck and cut it into portions. Season the duck with salt, pepper and herbs. Heat the oil in a deep, ovenproof casserole on top of the stove and brown the duck for 10 minutes. Add the apple juice and stock. Braise for 1 hour in the oven at 180 °C, then add the dried fruit and braise for a further 15 minutes. Transfer the duck and fruit to a deep dish while making the gravy. Mix the flour or cornflour and water to a paste and stir it into the pan juices. Heat the gravy, stirring, for 5 minutes on top of the stove and serve with the meat.

Serves 4–6

Braised Duck with Dried Fruit is a dish that successfully combines sweet and savoury flavours.

CHICKEN BREYANI

200 ml sunflower oil
12 medium onions, finely chopped
12 medium potatoes, cubed
600 g uncooked rice
250 ml red lentils, soaked and drained
10 ml salt
2 x 1.5 kg chickens, cut into portions
15 ml ground coriander
5 ml saffron or 10 ml turmeric
2 sticks cinnamon
4 bay or lemon leaves
10 cardamom seeds
5 ml cumin seeds
15 ml finely chopped chillies
3 large ripe tomatoes, skinned and
coarsely chopped
125 ml lemon juice
few black peppercorns
8 cloves garlic
500 ml natural yoghurt
2 pieces root ginger, crushed
8 hard-boiled eggs, shelled and
thinly sliced

Heat a little of the oil in a frying pan and sauté the onions for 5 minutes, or until transparent. Remove and set aside. Add the rest of the oil and the potatoes to the pan and sauté for about 8 minutes, or until lightly browned. Remove, drain on absorbent paper and set aside. Boil the rice in salted boiling water for 15 minutes, or until almost tender but still firm. Add more salt if necessary. Boil the lentils in salted water for 5 minutes, then drain. Combine the rice, lentils and a quarter of the fried onions. Rub the salt into the chicken pieces and place them in a large mixing bowl. Combine the coriander, saffron or turmeric, cinnamon, bay or lemon leaves, cardamom seeds, cumin seeds, chillies, tomatoes, lemon juice, peppercorns, remaining fried onion, garlic, yoghurt and ginger in a bowl. Pour over the chicken and leave for 30 minutes. Invert a large, heavy dinner plate in a large saucepan, covering the base completely. Arrange the ingredients on top in the following order: half the browned potatoes, sprinkled with 5 ml oil, chicken and marinade, eggs, rice and lentil mixture, remaining potatoes, remaining oil sprinkled over. Close the saucepan tightly and simmer, without stirring, for 1½ hours. Serve with sambals (see recipes on pages 76 and 77) of your choice.

Serves 10

NOTE: Breyani mix, available from supermarkets or specialist spice shops, may be used instead of mixing the individual spices.

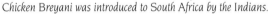

Chicken Breyani was introduced to South Africa by the Indians.

CHICKEN CURRY

This is based on an old Cape recipe, which used tamarind water instead of vinegar.

1.5–2 kg chicken
2t 10 ml salt
¼ut 2 ml milled pepper
200 ml dry white wine
125 ml water
5t 25 ml margarine, butter or chicken fat
1 large onion, chopped
little less than 1T (5t) 25 ml vinegar
1 large tart green apple, peeled, cored and grated
4t 20 ml curry powder
2t 10 ml sugar
1T 15 ml lemon juice
15 ml cake flour
1T

Cut the chicken into portions and season with salt and pepper. Place in a large saucepan, add the wine and water and simmer, covered, for 1–1½ hours, or until tender. Heat the margarine, butter or chicken fat in a frying pan and sauté the onion until transparent. Mix the vinegar, apple, curry powder and sugar, and add to the onion. Stir over moderate heat for 1–2 minutes, then add to the chicken. Bring to the boil and boil for 5 minutes. Mix the lemon juice and flour to a paste and stir into the chicken. Simmer for 5 minutes, then serve with rice topped with toasted flaked almonds and accompanied by sambals (see recipes on pages 76 and 77) of your choice.
Serves 6

MICROWAVE OVEN: Use the microwave oven to par-cook the chicken. Microwave at 100 per cent power for 6–7 minutes per 500 g. Transfer to a large saucepan, add the wine and water, and continue as described in the recipe above.

MALAY BRAISED CHICKEN

1.5 kg chicken, cut into portions
125 ml sunflower oil
2 potatoes, quartered
2 medium onions, finely chopped
200 ml water

MASALA
5 cloves garlic
1 piece root ginger
7 ml salt
5 ml crushed chillies
5 ml ground cumin
10 ml leaf masala
5 ml ground cloves
30 ml lemon juice
10 ml peri-peri sauce

First prepare the masala. Place the garlic, ginger and salt in a food processor or blender and process to a paste. Add the chillies, cumin, masala, cloves, lemon juice and peri-peri sauce and mix to a paste. Rub the mixture into the chicken portions and set them aside. Heat the oil in a large saucepan and sauté the potatoes for approximately 5 minutes on each side. Remove the potatoes from the oil, drain and set aside. Add the onions to the oil and sauté for about 5 minutes, or until they are transparent. Add the chicken and cook, turning occasionally, for approximately 15 minutes, or until it is well browned. Add the 200 ml water and cook for a further 10 minutes over moderate heat. Add the potatoes to the chicken mixture and simmer for about 15 minutes, or until the potatoes are tender. Serve with Yellow Rice with Raisins (page 72) and Mango Atjar (page 136).
Serves 6–8

Chicken for the pot
These days, the chickens available in supermarkets are fairly young – we can even buy very young *poussins* – so the flesh is tender and perfect for roasting in the oven or for grilling. The early colonists, however, tended to keep chickens until their laying days were over before cooking them, which meant that the flesh was too tough for a succulent roast. Such mature birds required long slow cooking, so braising and stewing were the favoured preparation methods.

CHAPTER 4

MEAT

There was already an abundance of beef at the Cape when the early settlers arrived, but the meat tended to be tough because the animals, having to range far and wide in search of food, developed muscle in the process. The fat-tailed sheep, however, provided flavourful mutton as a result of the veld bushes they fed on. There were plenty of wild animals and birds that yielded good meat and these were part of the daily diet from the start. Wild animals also formed a major part of the diet of those who trekked beyond the borders of the Cape Colony in later times, and many of the recipes for potjiekos stem from their experience (see Chapter 5). Pork and poultry were introduced by the colonists. Today the best mutton and lamb come from the Karoo or the grasslands of KwaZulu-Natal and the Free State. Many old recipes – those for bredies, for instance – call for fat mutton, but in our health-conscious era, less fatty lamb is preferred and mutton is not all that easy to find.

ROAST BEEF

The well-known 'roast beef of England' is, for many South Africans, the only meat to serve as the main meal on Sundays. At many country hotels you will still find that the main course at the main meal of the day – even during the week – is a roast.

1.5–2 kg beef for roasting
1 clove garlic, halved
10 ml salt
freshly milled black pepper
30 ml dripping

Preheat the oven to 220 °C. Wipe the beef, rub with cut garlic, season and place in a roasting pan with the dripping. Roast for 15 minutes, reduce the temperature to 190 °C and continue roasting for 15 minutes per 500 g for rare beef and 20 minutes per 500 g for medium rare. Remove the roast from the pan and set it aside to rest in the warming oven while you make the Meat Gravy (page 43) and Yorkshire Pudding (page 43). Serve, carved, with roast potatoes, gravy and Yorkshire pudding.
Serves 6

Roast Beef and Yorkshire Pudding are the traditional favourites for Sunday lunch.

FRIKKADELS (FRIKKADELLE)

Frikkadels, extremely popular in Holland in the 17th and 18th centuries, were introduced here by the Dutch settlers. In some form or other they remain favourites in many countries.

45 ml butter, margarine or sunflower oil
1 medium onion, minced or very finely chopped
750 g lean minced beef
1 thick slice crustless white bread, soaked in water and squeezed dry
2 large eggs
5 ml salt
1 ml milled pepper
1 ml ground allspice

Heat 15 ml of the butter, margarine or oil in a large frying pan and sauté the onion in it for about 5 minutes, or until transparent. Combine the onion with the mince, bread, eggs, salt, pepper and allspice, and shape into balls. Heat the remaining butter, margarine or oil in the frying pan, and brown the frikkadels, a few at a time, for about 5 minutes on one side. Turn them over and brown the other side, then turn down the heat slightly and continue cooking the frikkadels for about 10 minutes, or until cooked through. Serve hot with mashed potatoes and an onion and tomato sauce.
Serves 6–8

MICROWAVE OVEN: Frikkadels microwave very well, and turn brown during the standing time. Arrange half the frikkadels in a circle in a glass pie dish, cover them loosely with waxed paper and microwave at 100 percent power for 9–12 minutes. Leave to stand while microwaving the remaining frikkadels.

YORKSHIRE PUDDING

This is the traditional accompaniment to roast beef, and cooks claim that there is an art to making it correctly so that it does not first rise too much and then fall flat when taken from the oven. The secret is to make it while the meat is resting and to serve it immediately.

125 g bread flour
pinch of salt
1 large egg
150 ml milk
150 ml water
25 ml hot dripping from roast

Sift the flour and salt into a mixing bowl and make a well in the centre. Break the egg into the well and add the milk. Using an electric beater and mixing from the centre, gradually incorporate the flour into the liquid. Add a little water and beat until the batter is smooth and shiny. Stir in the remaining water. Spoon a little dripping into each cup of a patty pan. Heat until the dripping is smoking hot. Fill each cup with batter and bake the puddings on the top shelf of the oven at 200 °C for about 25 minutes, or until golden brown and well risen. Serve at once with the roast.
Serves 4–6

MEAT GRAVY

Gravies are generally made from pan scrapings and meat juices, mixed with water, thickening and seasoning. This applies to all kinds of meat.

dripping (fat and pan juices) from roast meat
15 ml cake flour
500 ml water
salt and milled pepper (optional)

Drain almost all the dripping from the roasting pan once the roast has been removed, leaving about 30 ml. Stir in the flour and cook the mixture gently over low heat until the flour is lightly browned. Remove from the stove and gradually blend in the water. When the mixture is smooth, return it to the stove and bring it to the boil, stirring. Add salt and pepper, if necessary, and pour the gravy into a gravy boat for serving.
Makes about 500 ml

CABBAGE FRIKKADELS (KOOLFRIKKADELLE)

These frikkadels, Malay in origin, are wrapped in blanched cabbage leaves and braised.

2 large onions, sliced
5 ml white sugar
butter, margarine or oil
2 cloves garlic, crushed
2 ml ground ginger
4 cardamom seeds, crushed
4 whole cloves
4 allspice berries
1 stick cinnamon, broken into pieces
3 large, ripe tomatoes, skinned and chopped
1 quantity Frikkadels (page 42)
1 large cabbage

Sauté the onions and sugar in heated butter, margarine or oil for about 5 minutes, or until transparent. With the saucepan still on the stove, add the garlic, ginger, cardamom seeds, cloves, allspice and cinnamon, and top with the tomatoes. Switch off the stove and set the mixture aside. Prepare the frikkadels as instructed in the recipe on page 42, but do not cook them. Meanwhile, remove the cabbage leaves from the head, wash well and place in a large dish. Pour boiling water over the leaves and leave them for a few minutes, until they are slightly softened but still crisp. Drain in a colander. Wrap each frikkadel in a cabbage leaf and pack them into the saucepan, on top of the onion and tomato mixture, with the seam side underneath. Switch on the stove and braise the frikkadels very slowly over low heat for about 45 minutes, or until the cabbage and meat are cooked and the onion and tomato mixture is delicately browned and cooked. Take care not to let the onions burn. Serve with cooked rice.
Serves 6–8

VARIATION: Instead of using cabbage leaves, try this traditional recipe. Blanch young and tender vine leaves in boiling water until softened and securely wrap smaller quantities of the frikkadel mixture in them. Continue as described in the recipe.

COTTAGE PIE

Also called Shepherd's pie, this British dish has been a favourite way of using up leftover meat in South Africa for countless generations.

30 ml sunflower oil
1 medium onion, finely chopped
350 g beef mince or minced leftover meat
2 medium ripe tomatoes, skinned and coarsely chopped
5 ml dried mixed herbs
salt and milled pepper
150 ml Meat (Beef) Stock (page 11)
500 g mashed potatoes
15 ml butter or margarine

Heat the oil and sauté the onion for approximately 5 minutes, or until transparent. If you are using uncooked beef mince, add it to the pan and brown it quickly on all sides. (If using cooked meat, add it after the tomatoes.) Add the tomatoes and heat through for about 3 minutes. Add the mixed herbs, salt, pepper and stock, stirring well. Place the meat mixture in a deep casserole and cover with the mashed potatoes. Dot the butter or margarine on top and bake the pie in the centre of the oven at 180 °C for approximately 40 minutes, or until it is crisp and brown on top. Serve with peas and butternut squash.

Serves 4

BRAAIED PORK SPARERIBS

Spareribs have become a popular item on the menus of many South African restaurants, but they are also delicious cooked over the coals for a family braai.

1.5 kg pork spareribs, washed and trimmed

MARINADE
125 ml soy sauce
25 ml honey
15 ml sherry
1 clove garlic, crushed

Place the spareribs in a shallow baking dish. Combine the ingredients for the marinade and pour over the ribs. Marinate for 2 hours, turning once. Drain, reserving the marinade. Braai the spareribs over moderate coals for 25–30 minutes, turning and basting often with the marinade.

Serves 6

VARIATION: Grill the marinated spareribs under a preheated grill for about 20 minutes, turning and basting often with the marinade.

SPIT-ROAST LAMB

An ox spit-roast over the coals was once the fare for a large gathering, and is still a custom in many parts of the country. This modern adaptation uses lamb, which takes much less time to cook.

about 16 kg lamb
salt and milled pepper

BASTING SAUCE
500 ml sunflower oil
100 ml lemon juice
3 cloves garlic, crushed
25 ml chopped fresh thyme
10 ml chopped fresh oregano
10 ml chopped fresh rosemary

Cut the lamb carcass open and spear it on the spit. Season the cavity with salt and pepper. Combine all the ingredients for the basting sauce. Braai the lamb over hot coals for about 3½–4 hours, or until done, basting often with the sauce.

Serves 20–30

NOTES
- If you do not have a spit braai, turn and baste the lamb often while it is cooking.
- As a spit takes a long time to braai, make a second fire to supply hot coals when needed.

BOBOTIE

The bobotie we know today was also popular in Europe in the Middle Ages, after the Crusaders introduced turmeric from the East. Bobotie is traditionally made with meat left over from the Sunday roast.

1 slice white bread
250 ml milk
1 kg lean minced beef or mutton
1 medium onion, peeled and
** finely chopped**
125 ml seedless raisins
125 ml blanched almonds
15 ml smooth apricot jam
15 ml fruit chutney
25 ml lemon juice
5 ml chopped fresh mixed herbs
10 ml curry powder
5 ml turmeric
10 ml salt
10 ml sunflower oil
3 large eggs
4 bay or lemon leaves

Soak the bread in 125 ml milk, then squeeze it dry and reserve the milk. Mix the bread with the minced beef or mutton. Mix in all the other ingredients, except the remaining and reserved milk, the oil, eggs and bay or lemon leaves. Heat the oil in a frying pan and brown the meat mixture lightly. Turn it out into a casserole. Beat the eggs with the remaining and reserved milk, and pour the mixture over the meat. Garnish the top of the mixture with the bay or lemon leaves and bake at 180 °C for approximately 50 minutes, or until set. Serve with Yellow Rice with Raisins (page 72).
Serves 6–8

Bobotie, Yellow Rice with Raisins (page 72) and Cabbage Frikkadels (page 42).

Pannas
In the early days at the Cape, the colonists made a kind of blood pudding, called pannas, from the lightly fried liver and kidneys of a pig. Tamarind water was added to sour it, and it was covered with fat before baking. To lengthen the storage time, it was covered with melted butter. The settlers served it sliced and fried in fat. It is still made today in some regions, most notably in Calvinia.

BAKED HAM

Baked, glazed ham has always had a pride of place on the Christmas dinner table, and it is certainly one of the easiest, and tastiest, treats at this time of year.

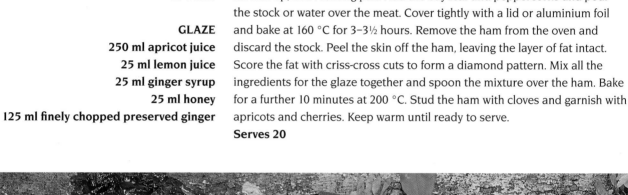

5 kg cured ham or gammon
5 ml mustard powder
10 ml ground ginger
1 bay leaf
5 peppercorns
500 ml Vegetable Stock (page 12)
or water

GLAZE
250 ml apricot juice
25 ml lemon juice
25 ml ginger syrup
25 ml honey
125 ml finely chopped preserved ginger

GARNISH
10 cloves
410 g can apricot halves, drained
410 g can stoned cherries, drained

Dust the ham or gammon with mustard powder and ground ginger. Place, fat side up, in a roasting pan. Add the bay leaf and peppercorns and pour the stock or water over the meat. Cover tightly with a lid or aluminium foil and bake at 160 °C for 3–3½ hours. Remove the ham from the oven and discard the stock. Peel the skin off the ham, leaving the layer of fat intact. Score the fat with criss-cross cuts to form a diamond pattern. Mix all the ingredients for the glaze together and spoon the mixture over the ham. Bake for a further 10 minutes at 200 °C. Stud the ham with cloves and garnish with apricots and cherries. Keep warm until ready to serve.
Serves 20

Baked Ham, Watercress Salad (page 75) and Onion Salad (page 76).

ROAST SUCKING PIG

Our ancestors roasted sucking pigs on a spit over the open fire. This recipe is for oven roasting.

1 sucking pig
25 ml salt
10 ml milled pepper
250 g butter or fat
500 ml boiling water
2 large apples
honey mixed with ground ginger, or
smooth apricot jam mixed with
brown sugar

Clean and weigh the pig. Calculate 50 minutes roasting time per 500 g meat. Make 4 skin-deep incisions, each about 7 cm long, on either side of and at right angles to the backbone. Place the pig on the rack of a roasting pan and rub it with salt, pepper and butter or fat. Place an apple in the pig's mouth. Add the boiling water and cover the pig with foil, adding an extra layer over the ears and feet to prevent burning or overcooking. Roast at 230 °C for 15 minutes, then lower the temperature to 150 °C and continue roasting the pig for the calculated time. (The meat is done when the internal temperature reads 100 °C on a meat thermometer.) Remove the foil after 2½ hours and spread the honey and ginger or apricot jam and brown sugar over the skin. Roast, uncovered, for the rest of the roasting time. Serve it whole on a platter, with a fresh apple in its mouth.
Serves 20–30

VARIATION: To braai on a spit, cover the nose, ears and feet with foil and baste the pig often with a mixture of water, oil and herbs of your choice as it braais.

ROAST LEG OF LAMB

50 ml fresh white breadcrumbs
50 ml softened butter
juice and grated rind of 1 small lemon
3 cloves garlic, crushed
10 ml chopped fresh rosemary
2.5–3 kg leg of lamb
15 ml salt
10 ml milled pepper

Combine the breadcrumbs, butter, lemon juice and rind, garlic and rosemary. Sprinkle the lamb with salt and pepper, and spread the breadcrumb mixture over it. Place on a rack in a roasting pan and cover loosely with foil. Roast at 180 °C for 25 minutes per 500 g meat. Remove the foil and roast for a further 15 minutes. Serve sliced, with rice or roast potatoes.
Serves 6

DENNINGVLEIS

Goat's meat was often used in spicy stews like this one. The Malay name means 'flavoured meat'.

15 ml dripping or sunflower oil
2 cloves garlic, crushed
2 large onions, sliced
10 ml white sugar
1 kg mutton rib or stewing mutton, cubed
4 whole cloves
4 allspice berries
2 bay or lemon leaves
5 ml salt
milled pepper
2 ml freshly grated nutmeg
125 ml water
2 ml tamarind seeds soaked in
125 ml water, or 50 ml brown vinegar
or lemon juice

Heat the dripping or oil in a large saucepan and sauté the garlic, onions and sugar for about 5 minutes, or until the onions are transparent. Remove the mixture from the saucepan and set aside. Brown the meat in the same saucepan. Add the onion mixture, the cloves, allspice, bay or lemon leaves, salt, pepper, nutmeg and water. Simmer, covered, for 1½ hours, or until the meat is tender. Strain the tamarind water and discard the seeds. Add the tamarind water, vinegar or lemon juice to the stew. Simmer for another 15 minutes. Serve with boiled potatoes.
Serves 6

NOTES
• Tamarind seeds are available from specialist spice shops. They impart a slightly sour flavour and can be used instead of vinegar.
• Goat's meat is similar to mutton, but it is more strongly flavoured.

LAMB CURRY

Our ancestors would have used mutton to make a curry, but modern awareness of more healthy eating has swung the focus away from fatty mutton to leaner lamb. The combination of sweet and savoury – achieved by adding dried peaches, apricots, or raisins – in dishes like curries and Bobotie (page 45) is peculiarly South African, a legacy of the Malay cooks who adapted oriental recipes and used local ingredients to create a new culinary tradition.

1.5T 25 ml sunflower oil
2 large onions, finely chopped
1 bay leaf
.6t 2 ml ground cinnamon
1t 5 ml ground coriander
.6t 2 ml ground cumin
2 cloves garlic crushed
4t 20 ml curry powder
6t 25 ml cake flour
1t 5 ml turmeric
1.5 kg lamb rib, trimmed of excess fat and cubed
500 g medium tomatoes, skinned and chopped
6–8 dried peaches or apricots, finely chopped

30 ml Fruit Chutney (page 136)
250 ml Meat (Beef) Stock (page 11)
5 ml white sugar 1t
10 ml salt 2t
milled black pepper

Heat the oil in a large saucepan and sauté the onions for about 5 minutes, or until transparent. Add the bay leaf, cinnamon, coriander, cumin, garlic, curry powder, flour and turmeric, and simmer for a few minutes, stirring constantly. Add the meat and brown it lightly, adding a little more oil if necessary. Add the remaining ingredients and mix well. Simmer over moderate heat for 1 hour. Serve immediately with boiled rice and bowls of sliced banana, desiccated coconut, diced pineapple and chutney.
Serves 6

VARIATION: Use mutton instead of lamb.

SOSATIES

Sosaties – skewered meat marinated in a curry sauce – formed part of the rijsttafel of Java, an elaborate banquet which always included at least two meat dishes, one fish course and a curry dish, as well as several vegetables, served on cooked rice and mixed with a strong curry sauce. Today we tend to cook sosaties over the coals, and any braai cook worth his or her salt has a 'secret recipe' for the marinade.

MARINADE
75 ml smooth apricot jam
25 ml brown sugar
3 cloves garlic, crushed
15 ml cornflour
2 bay or lemon leaves
25 ml curry powder
25 ml wine vinegar
10 ml salt
5 ml milled pepper

SOSATIES
3 medium onions, quartered
1.5 kg leg of lamb, cut into 2.5 cm cubes

1 kg pork, cubed
250 g dried apricots
125 ml cubed mutton fat

Combine all the ingredients for the marinade in a saucepan and add the onion quarters. Bring to the boil and boil for 5 minutes, or until slightly thickened, stirring occasionally. Transfer the marinade to a large dish. Add the lamb and pork cubes and marinate them for 4 hours (or overnight) in a cool place, turning them 2–3 times. Soak the apricots in water to cover until plump, then drain. Remove the meat from the marinade and thread it into skewers alternatively with the mutton fat, apricots and onion. Braai the sosaties over moderate coals, or grill in the oven, turning frequently, for 25 minutes, or until cooked. Serve with Crumbly Mealie Porridge (page 74)
Serves 6–8

Sosaties and Lamb Curry are two delectable ways to add a piquant flavour to meat.

PUMPKIN BREDIE

Bredies are stews made from meat and vegetables which are cooked very slowly to allow the flavour of the ingredients to merge completely. Almost any vegetable can be used to make bredies, but traditionally the only meat used was fat mutton rib. Because bredies require long, slow cooking, they're ideal for cooking in a cast-iron pot over the coals.

25 ml butter, margarine, lard or sunflower oil
2 large onions, sliced
1 clove garlic, crushed
1 kg stewing lamb or mutton, cubed
10 ml salt
milled black pepper
100 ml stock, water or wine
500 g potatoes, sliced
2 kg pumpkin, peeled, seeded and cubed
1 small piece root ginger, crushed
10 ml brown sugar
5 ml ground cinnamon

Heat the butter, margarine, lard or oil in a large saucepan and sauté the onions and garlic for about 5 minutes, or until the onions are transparent. Add the meat and brown the cubes quickly on all sides. Add the salt, pepper and stock, water or wine and simmer, covered, for 1½–2 hours, or until the meat starts to get tender. Add the potatoes, pumpkin, ginger, brown sugar and ground cinnamon, and stew for 1 hour longer. Serve with cooked rice.
Serves 6

WATERBLOMMETJIE BREDIE

Waterblommetjies (Aponogeton distachyos) are gathered in spring along waterways in the Cape Peninsula and Boland. When it is waterblommetjie time, you'll see the hawkers alongside the road, with packets of the famous water plant for sale. Don't use the plants for cooking if they still have their small whites flowers; they are still immature and will merely cook away to a pulp.

30 ml butter, margarine, lard or sunflower oil
2 large onions, sliced
1 clove garlic, crushed
1.5 kg mutton or lamb rib, cubed
200 ml water
10 ml salt
800 g waterblommetjies, trimmed and soaked in salt water
1 tart green apple, peeled and grated, or 1 bunch sorrel, chopped
500 g potatoes, cubed
200 ml dry white wine
milled black pepper
freshly grated nutmeg

Heat the butter, margarine, lard or oil in a large saucepan and sauté the onions and the garlic for 5 minutes, or until the onions are transparent. Add the meat and brown it quickly, then add the water and salt. Simmer, covered, for 1½–2 hours or until the meat becomes tender. Drain the waterblommetjies and add them to the saucepan with the apple or sorrel, potatoes and wine. Simmer, covered, for a further 30 minutes. Season with pepper and nutmeg and serve with rice, garnished with lemon slices.

Serves 6

VARIATION: To make cabbage bredie, substitute shredded cabbage for the waterblommetjies, use 250 ml chopped celery and 5 ml chopped fresh dill instead of the apple, and use only about a quarter of the liquid. Proceed as in the recipe above.

Clockwise from top left: Bean Bredie, Waterblommetjie Bredie and Tomato Bredie.

VELDKOOL BREDIE

Our forefathers used many wild plants from the veld, mainly in stews. Wild asparagus (veldkool), gathered along the West Coast in early spring, adds a piquant flavour to this bredie.

25 ml sunflower oil
2 medium onions, sliced
2 cloves garlic, crushed
2.5 kg mutton neck or stewing
lamb, cubed
250 ml Meat (Beef) Stock (page 11)
10 ml salt
2 ml milled pepper
2 kg veldkool (wild asparagus),
rinsed well

5 medium potatoes, sliced
10 ml lemon juice

Heat the oil in a large saucepan and sauté the onions and garlic for about 5 minutes, or until the onions are transparent. Add the meat and brown lightly on all sides. Add the stock, salt and pepper and simmer, covered, for 1½–2 hours, or until the meat is tender. Add the veldkool and potatoes, and simmer for about 30–45 minutes. Stir in the lemon juice and serve the bredie with cooked rice.

Serves 6

TOMATO BREDIE

We ate a lot of bredies when I was a child. Tomato bredie was usually served on a Monday, with cooked rice and a green salad.

25 ml butter, margarine, lard or
sunflower oil
2 large onions, sliced
1 clove garlic, crushed
1.5 kg stewing lamb or mutton, cubed
10 ml salt
milled pepper
little stock, water or wine
500 g potatoes, sliced
1 kg medium tomatoes, skinned
and chopped
5 ml white sugar

2 ml dried thyme
5 ml chopped fresh marjoram

Heat the butter, margarine, lard or sunflower oil in a large saucepan and sauté the onions and garlic for about 5 minutes, or until the onions are transparent. Add the meat and brown quickly on all sides. Add the salt, pepper and a little stock, water or wine and simmer, covered, for 1½–2 hours, or until the meat starts to get tender. Add the potatoes, tomatoes, sugar, thyme and marjoram, and stew for a further hour. Serve with cooked rice.

Serves 6

BEAN BREDIE

We always called this Thursday bredie, because that's the day my mother made it.

25 ml butter, margarine, lard or
sunflower oil
2 large onions, sliced
1 clove garlic, crushed
1 kg mutton neck or stewing lamb, cubed
250 ml stock, water or wine
1 kg green beans, topped and tailed
and sliced
2 large potatoes, sliced
5 ml salt
5 ml chopped fresh marjoram

milled pepper
freshly grated nutmeg

Heat the butter, margarine, lard or oil in a large saucepan and sauté the onions and garlic for about 5 minutes, or until the onions are transparent. Add the meat and brown on all sides. Add the stock, water or wine and simmer, covered, for about 1½–2 hours, or until the meat becomes tender. Add the beans, potatoes, salt, marjoram and pepper, and continue cooking for 30–45 minutes, or until the beans are tender. Grate nutmeg over and serve with rice.

Serves 6

OXTAIL STEW

Of British origin, this stew has become a favourite in this country. I know one aficionado who tries oxtail wherever it is offered on the menu, and keeps a record of the relative merits of each offering.

1.5 kg oxtail, trimmed and cut into joints
1 clove garlic, crushed
500 ml Meat (Beef) Stock (page 11)
1 bay leaf
4 whole cloves
5 peppercorns
5 ml salt
5 ml milled pepper
1 medium onion, sliced, or
    10 pickling onions, peeled
8–10 young carrots

Place the meat, garlic, 250 ml of the stock, the bay leaf, cloves, peppercorns, salt and pepper in a heavy-based saucepan. Simmer, covered, over moderate heat for 3–4 hours, adding more boiling stock as needed. After 2 hours of cooking, add the onion and carrots. Remove the cloves and bay leaf, and skim off the fat before serving with boiled or mashed potatoes.
Serves 4–6

NOTE: Oxtail stew is perfect for cooking in a potjie over the coals.

Oxtail Stew makes a mouthwatering meal, especially in the heart of winter.

BRAISED LIVER WITH ONIONS

Offal is an important part of the Malay menu, and they often serve liver braised with onions. The secret of tender braised liver is to cut it thinly and cook it quickly.

65 ml sunflower oil
750 g calf's liver, skinned and thinly sliced
3 medium onions, sliced
salt and milled pepper
45–60 ml Meat (Beef) Stock (page 11) or water

Heat a little of the oil and fry the liver quickly on both sides. Set the liver aside and keep it warm. Heat the rest of the oil in the pan and sauté the onions for about 5 minutes, or until transparent. Season lightly with salt and pepper and add the stock or water to the pan. Cook, uncovered, over high heat until slightly reduced, then return the liver to the pan and heat through for 5–10 minutes over moderate heat. Serve immediately with mashed potatoes.
Serves 6

BILTONG

Biltong (savoury dried meat) has been around for centuries; for instance, a more primitive form, the Dutch tassal, was also prepared in certain areas of France during the late Middle Ages. Tassal was also made in Batavia, and made its way to South Africa with the Dutch settlers, where it was adapted to the less pungent biltong. Most farmers still have a special rack where they hang the biltong to dry.

12.5 kg venison, beef or ostrich meat (fillet, rump or sirloin)
560 g fine salt
125 ml brown sugar
25 ml bircarbonate of soda
10 ml saltpetre (optional)
12.5 ml milled pepper
125 ml coarsely ground coriander
250 ml brown vinegar
2.5 litres warm water

Cut the meat along the natural dividing lines of the muscles down the length of the whole leg, or a portion of it. Cut the pieces into strips of about 5–7 cm thick, with some fat on each strip. Mix the salt, sugar, bicarbonate of soda (this makes the biltong tender), saltpetre, pepper and coriander together, and rub the mixture into the strips of meat. Layer the meat – with the more bulky pieces at the bottom – in a wooden, earthenware, plastic or enamel container and sprinkle a little vinegar over each layer. Leave the meat in a cool place for about 1–2 days, depending on how thick the meat is and how salty you want it to be. Mix the vinegar and water and dip the biltong into it (this makes it shiny and dark). Pat the pieces of meat dry and hang them on S-shaped hooks – or use pieces of string – about 5 cm apart (so that the air can circulate freely among the strips of meat) in a cool, airy place. Leave for 2–3 weeks until the biltong is dry.
Makes about 10 kg

DRIED SAUSAGE (DROËWORS)

3 kg beef
20 ml salt
2 ml pepper
50 ml ground roasted coriander
2 ml ground allspice
2 ml ground cloves
500 g mutton tail fat

25 ml brown vinegar
85 g sausage casings

Season the meat with the salt, pepper and spices. Mince all the ingredients (except the casings) together coarsely. Press the mixture loosely into the casings and hang the sausage up to dry in a cold, dry place, ensuring that the sausages are protected from flies and dust. Leave to dry for 2–3 weeks.
Makes about 2.5 kg

SALTED RIB (SOUTRIBBETJIE)

Ribs, given a similar treatment to biltong, are really delicious braaied over the coals.

20 ml brown sugar
250 ml coarse salt
2 ml saltpetre
10 ml ground coriander
5 ml ground cloves
20 ml brown vinegar
2 kg flat rib or breast of lamb

Combine the sugar, salt, saltpetre, coriander, cloves and vinegar. Rub well into the meat. Place the meat in a plastic, glass or earthenware container and refrigerate for 2 days. Remove the rib and hang it in a cool, airy place to dry. Grill or braai the rib for 30 minutes, turning often, or until done to taste.
Serves 6

Dried meat
Salting or pickling (curing) meat was the traditional means of preserving it before there were refrigerators and freezers in which to store the food. Each of the ingredients used for preserving had a special role to play: salt preserved the meat, saltpetre imparted the colour and prevented decay, sugar kept the meat from drying out too much and spices added flavour.

HOME-MADE BOEREWORS

Our self-sufficient farming community wasted nothing. When a beast was slaughtered in winter, all parts were used, including the trotters, which were used for making Brawn (page 59), and the intestines, which were used as casings for home-made sausage. Every farmer's wife prided herself on her own special recipe for making sausage. The fillings ranged from beef and mutton to game meat or even game offal encased in game intestines and called Skilpad and Pofadder (page 67).

1.5 kg beef
1.5 kg pork
500 g speck, diced
25 ml salt
5 ml milled pepper
50 ml ground coriander
2 ml freshly grated nutmeg
1 ml ground cloves
2 ml ground dried thyme
2 ml ground allspice
125 ml brown vinegar
1 clove garlic, crushed
50 ml Worcestershire sauce
85 g sausage casings

Mince or process the meat coarsely, then mix it with all the other ingredients, except the sausage casings. Fill the sausage casings firmly but not too tightly with the meat mixture, making sure that the speck is distributed evenly throughout the sausage. Boerewors can be fried, grilled or braaied over the coals. It will keep in the refrigerator for 1–2 days and in the freezer for up to 3 months.
Makes 3.5 kg

VARIATIONS: Use veal, lamb or venison instead of beef.

TRIPE AND TROTTERS (PENS-EN-POOTJIES)

This dish is part of many a culinary culture, including that of the Malay community. Another popular way to cook tripe is in buttermilk, which tenderizes the tripe.

4 sheep's trotters, cleaned and chopped
1 sheep's tripe, cleaned
salted water
25 ml brown vinegar
5 ml white sugar
2 whole cloves
10 ml peppercorns
5 ml coriander seeds
5 ml allspice berries
1 bay leaf
10 ml salt
2 ml milled pepper
1 large onion, sliced
15 ml curry powder
10 ml turmeric
500 g small potatoes

Soak the trotters and tripe in enough salted water to cover for 1 hour. Drain. Boil each separately in enough fresh cold water to cover for about 1 hour, or until soft. Drain, reserving the liquid from the trotters. Dice the meat, add the reserved liquid and all the other ingredients and simmer, covered, for about 45 minutes. Serve with boiled rice.
Serves 6

SAMOOSAS

Samoosas are a favourite among many South Africans.

Samoosas were introduced to South Africa by Indian immigrants, and have also been adopted by the Malay community and become a favoured snack of many other South Africans. The pastry triangles can have a filling of meat or vegetables.

DOUGH
375 g cake flour
5 ml salt
250 ml cold water
5 ml lemon juice
15 ml melted butter or sunflower oil

FILLING
500 g mutton or lamb, minced
2 ml turmeric
5 ml salt
1 large clove garlic
1 piece root ginger
10 ml finely chopped coriander leaves
1 green chilli, crushed
2 medium onions, finely chopped
15 ml melted butter
4 spring onions, finely chopped
2 ml garam masala

sunflower oil

To make the dough, sift the flour and salt together and add enough cold water to make a stiff dough. Add the lemon juice and knead the dough gently until elastic. Divide the dough into 12 pieces and roll each into a ball. Roll out 6 balls on a floured surface and shape them into 10-cm diameter rounds. Brush each with melted butter or oil and sprinkle with flour. Stack the rounds, leaving the final round ungreased and unfloured. Roll out the stack into a large, very thin round and trim the sides to form a square. Heat an ungreased baking sheet in the oven at 230 °C until very hot, remove and place the dough square on it. Turn the square over several time until the dough puffs up slightly. Remove the square from the baking sheet as soon as this happens. Repeat for the remaining 6 balls of dough.

To make the filling, cook the meat with a mixture of the turmeric, salt, garlic and ginger pounded together, the coriander leaves and the chillies. When nearly dry, add the onions and cook until the liquid has evaporated, stirring often to prevent lumps forming. Add the melted butter, allow the mixture to cool and add the spring onions and garam masala.

To assemble, cut the prepared dough squares into strips 8 cm wide and 25–30 cm long. Separate into layers before the pastry cools. (Cover them with a damp cloth to prevent drying out while making the samoosas.) Holding a strip of pastry in your left hand, pull the bottom corner across, then fold it up to form a triangle with sharp corners and a pocket in which to put the filling. Fill with 10 ml filling, then continue folding the pastry across the top of the triangle to seal off the opening. Tuck the edges round to form a neat triangle. Seal the remaining edge with a paste of flour and water, and pinch the two bottom edges lightly together. Leave in a cool place for about 30 minutes before cooking. Fry the samoosas in hot oil for about 10 minutes, or until golden, turning often. Remove and drain in a colander or on absorbent paper.
Serves 6-8

SMOKING MEAT

Our farming ancestors used to smoke meat in special smoke-houses. Today, there's a much quicker method, called smoke roasting, which does not require the meat to be soaked in brine beforehand. Smoking may also be done over hot coals, in a commercial smoker or in a closed braai like the Weber braai.

YOU WILL NEED:
- A heavy-based saucepan with a tight-fitting lid.
- A trivet or pot stand that will fit inside the saucepan (this allows the air to circulate all round the food to be smoked).
- A metal container for the food, which fits inside the saucepan but still allows air to circulate freely. A foil dish is the easiest alternative.
- Untreated hardwood shavings – oak is generally best – available from hardware stores. Use only 30 ml per saucepan, otherwise the meat will be bitter.

HERE'S HOW TO SMOKE MEAT:
- Sprinkle the wood shavings in the base of the saucepan and place the trivet in the saucepan.
- Brush the meat with oil and season as desired.
- Place on the foil plate and position the plate on the trivet in the saucepan.
- Close the saucepan tightly – if the lid doesn't seal properly, place aluminium foil over the saucepan and jam the lid on.
- Cook (smoke) the meat on top of the stove, on high, for 15 minutes, then reduce the temperature to low and smoke the meat for an additional 30 minutes for rare beef fillet, or 1 hour for pork, lamb or medium to well-done beef fillet.
- Some smoked meats, like beef, require additional curing. To do this, wrap the meat in foil and, when cooled, refrigerate for 24 hours.
- Smoke boerewors for 15 minutes on high, and 15 minutes on low. Serve hot or cold.
- Pork and lamb may be used right after smoking, or cured for a further 24 hours and served cold.
- Meat can be smoked until it is completely done, or smoked until half done and then roasted.

STEAK AND KIDNEY PIE

250 g Shortcrust Pastry (page 100)

FILLING
25 ml sunflower oil
750 g stewing steak, cubed
2 lamb's kidneys, cleaned and diced
1 large onion, chopped
250 ml Meat (Beef) Stock (page 11)
5 ml salt
2 ml milled pepper
25 ml cake flour

To make the filling, heat the oil in a frying pan and brown the steak and kidneys on all sides. Add the onion and sauté for about 5 minutes, or until the onion is transparent. Add the stock, salt and pepper and simmer, covered, for 1½–2 hours. Mix the flour to a paste with a little water and use to thicken the gravy. Spoon the mixture into a deep pie dish and leave it to cool slightly. Roll the pastry out and use to cover the meat, crimping the edges to the rim of the pie dish. Cut slits in the top of the crust to allow steam to escape during the cooking and bake the pie at 200 °C for 15 minutes.
Serves 6

SAVOURY TART (SOUTTERT)

In many South African homes, no family gathering would be complete without a delectable savoury tart – and, of course, a melktert (see Milk Tart, page 101).

250 g Shortcrust Pastry (page 100)

FILLING
30 ml cornflour
500 ml milk
4 large eggs, beaten
3 rashers rindless bacon, chopped
2 slices ham, cubed
**5 slices salami, smoked sausage or
    chopped Vienna sausages**
30 ml finely chopped onion
30 ml finely chopped fresh parsley
250 ml grated Cheddar cheese
**30 ml seeded and chopped green
    sweet pepper**

Line a large pie dish with the pastry. To make the filling, combine the cornflour and the milk, then stir in the remaining ingredients, mixing well. Pour the filling into the pastry shell and bake the tart at 180 °C for 25 minutes, or until the pastry is golden and the filling has set. Serve hot.
Serves 6–8

Savoury Tart is a firm favourite at family gatherings.

LAMB PIE (RUGSTRINGPASTEI)

Curried Mince Pies and Lamb Pie were popular in Holland in the seventeenth century.

250 g Puff Pastry (page 100)

FILLING
25 ml sunflower oil
1 onion, sliced
1 kg stewing lamb or chine, cubed
8 whole cloves
1 bay leaf
10 ml salt
250 ml water
2 rashers bacon, chopped
5 ml chopped fresh rosemary
25 ml cake flour
2 hard-boiled eggs, shelled and sliced

To make the filling, heat the oil in a frying pan and sauté the onion for about 5 minutes, or until transparent. Add the meat and brown quickly on all sides. Add the cloves, bay leaf, salt and water, and stew the meat for about 1 hour, or until very soft. Remove the meat from the bones, if desired. Roll out half the puff pastry and use it to line a pie dish. Add the bacon, rosemary and flour to the meat. Spoon the meat mixture into the pie dish and arrange the egg slices on top. Roll out the remaining pastry and cover the meat with it, crimping the pastry edges together. Cut slits in the crust to allow steam to escape during cooking and bake at 230 °C for 10 minutes. Reduce the heat to 180 °C and bake for a further 20–30 minutes.

Serves 6

CURRIED MINCE PIES

In the days before refrigeration, curry was often used to make meat last longer. These pies are a perfect example.

350 g Flaky or Shortcrust Pastry (page 100), without sugar

FILLING
1 slice white bread
50 ml milk
½ medium onion, finely chopped
15 ml sunflower oil
10 ml medium-strength curry powder
500 g minced lean beef
5 ml chutney
5 ml salt
milled black pepper
10 ml lemon juice or brown vinegar
1 large egg, beaten

To make the filling, soak the bread in the milk. Sauté the onion in heated oil for 5 minutes, or until the onion is transparent. Add the curry powder and fry for a few minutes. Add the meat and chutney and cook for 5 minutes, or until the meat is browned. Add the remaining seasoning and simmer for another 5 minutes. Allow the mixture to cool, then mix it with the soaked bread. Roll out the pastry and cut out 24 rounds with a biscuit cutter. Place spoonfuls of filling in the centre of 12 rounds and brush the edges of the pastry with cold water. Cover each round with a second round and press the edges together with a fork. Prick the top crust to allow steam to escape during baking. Brush with beaten egg and place the pies on a baking sheet. Bake at 200 °C for 20 minutes, or until the pastry is golden. Serve hot.
Makes about 12

TRADITIONAL BRAWN

Brawn was part of the Christmas fare in Europe during the Middle Ages. It was made from wild boar, and ale or wine was often part of the recipe. Early settlers in South Africa continued the tradition, substituting the locally available meat for the more exotic boar. All the scraps of meat left over when an animal was slaughtered went into the brawn, so nothing was wasted.

12 sheep's trotters
125 g lime dissolved in 9 litres boiling water
4 whole cloves
12 allspice berries
12 black peppercorns
15 ml coriander seeds
4 bay leaves
250 ml brown vinegar
10 ml salt

Dip the trotters in the lime water and scrape them clean. Soak them in salted water to cover for 1 hour. Drain and chop the trotters into small pieces. Cover with fresh water and simmer over low heat until the meat is tender. Remove the bones. Tie the cloves, allspice berries, peppercorns, coriander seeds and bay leaves in a muslin bag and add to the saucepan. Add the vinegar and salt and simmer, covered, for 1 hour. Remove the bag of spices. Spray a mould or glass dish with non-stick cooking spray and pour in the mixture. Chill until set and serve cold. Brawn will keep for about 1 week if refrigerated. Do not freeze, as the texture of the jelly is spoilt by freezing and thawing.
Serves 10

CHAPTER 5

GAME AND GAME BIRDS

The hunters and settlers of the earlier days were, of necessity, outdoor cooks. They had few utensils – the cast-iron potjie was essential – but they put them to good use to cook whatever they caught or shot. For some game, like porcupine, they patted wet clay or a plain flour and water dough around the animal, skin and all (but they removed the quills), then made a hole in the hot coals, placed the parcel in it and covered it with hot coals. The meat cooked slowly for a couple of hours, until succulent and tender. When done, the clay or dough was cracked open and the skin came away with it, leaving the beautifully cooked meat. Game birds like Muscovy duck, guineafowl and pheasant require long, slow cooking because they do not have much fat on them. They were traditionally pot-roasted and braised, and often used in stews cooked over the coals or on top of the stove.

VENISON PIE

The Dutch love of pies has become a South African tradition as well.

500 g Flaky Pastry (page 100)

FILLING
1 kg cooked venison, cubed
200 g rindless streaky bacon, chopped
15 ml chutney
125 g dried apricots, chopped
30 ml red wine
5 ml chopped fresh thyme
1 clove garlic, crushed

Halve the pastry. Roll out one half and use to line a pie dish. Combine all the ingredients for the filling and spoon the mixture into the pie dish. Cover with rolled-out reserved pastry and crimp the edges together. Cut slits in the top to allow steam to escape during baking. Bake at 180 °C for 30 minutes, or until the pastry is crisp and golden. Serve with Yellow Rice with Raisins (page 72) and Quince Jelly (page 130).
Serves 8

Venison Pie (top) and Pot-roast Venison with Stuffed Baked Apples (page 85) and Vegetable Curry (page 73).

VENISON SAUSAGE

The fat in the tail of the fat-tailed sheep, once common all over the country, was a great cooking and household aid for the farmer's wife. It added just the right flavour to all sorts of home-made sausages.

500 g mutton tail fat (see Note)
2 kg venison, without sinews and membranes
1 kg pork
5 ml ground cloves
15 ml salt
50 ml crushed coriander seeds
2 ml finely chopped fresh thyme
1 thick slice white bread, toasted
50 ml dry red wine
50 ml brown vinegar
60 g sausage casings

Cube 250 g of tail fat and set aside. Mince the venison, pork and remaining tail fat with the cloves, salt, coriander and thyme. Mince the bread separately. Combine the meat mixture with the fat, bread, wine and vinegar. Stuff the filling into the casings, making sure that the fat is evenly distributed.
Makes 3.5–4 kg

NOTE: If you freeze the tail fat before mincing and cubing, it will be much easier to work with. Make sure that the fat is evenly distributed in the sausages.

POT-ROAST VENISON

Game meat is lean, and needs additional fat and long cooking to become tender. Farm-reared game is now available from butchers in some centres.

250 g speck, cut into thin strips
30 ml brown vinegar
5 ml salt
5 ml brown sugar
2–2.5 kg leg of venison
100 g seedless raisins
2 cloves garlic, cut into slivers
2 ml milled pepper
2 ml ground ginger
20 ml salt
20 ml brown sugar
1 medium onion, sliced
1 bay leaf
6 whole cloves
500 ml dry red wine
250 ml red wine vinegar
30 ml fat or sunflower oil
30 ml cake flour
60 ml smooth apricot jam
60 ml medium cream sherry

Marinate the speck for 45 minutes in the vinegar mixed with the 5 ml salt and 5 ml sugar. Drain and reserve the liquid. Freeze the speck strips (they are then easier to handle). Pierce the venison with a sharp knife and place a raisin, sliver of garlic and strip of speck in each incision. Rub the pepper, ginger, 20 ml salt and 20 ml sugar into the meat. Place it in a large earthenware or glass dish with the onion slices, bay leaf, cloves, reserved liquid, wine and red wine vinegar, and marinate for 2–3 days, turning twice a day. Heat the fat or oil in a heavy-based saucepan and brown the drained meat, turning often. Add 250 ml of the marinade and simmer for 2–3 hours, or until tender. Add more marinade if it becomes too dry. Mix the flour, jam and sherry to a paste and use it to baste the meat. Roast for a further 5 minutes. Serve with stewed dried fruit, Baked Quinces (page 86), Stuffed Baked Apples (page 85) or Yellow Rice with Raisins (page 72).
Serves 8

VARIATIONS
- Use dried apricot slices instead of raisins.
- Prepare and marinate the meat as for pot-roast venison, then place the meat in an ovenproof dish and roast, covered with foil, for 2–3 hours at 160 °C, basting often. Remove the foil for the last 15 minutes of roasting time to brown the meat.

BAKED PHEASANT

Our great-grandmothers used this recipe to cook all kinds of game birds. If pheasant is not available, guineafowl can also be used.

2 kg pheasant, skinned
65 ml cake flour seasoned with 5 ml
each salt and milled pepper
25 ml lard or butter
1 large onion, thinly sliced
170 g rindless bacon, diced
1 small cabbage, shredded
150 g small carrots
125 g fresh green peas
170 g stoned prunes, soaked overnight
in water to cover
125 ml red wine
4 smoked sausages

Roll the pheasant in the seasoned flour. Melt the lard or butter in a large frying pan and brown the pheasant until golden, turning occasionally to brown all over. Remove the bird from the pan. Add the onion and bacon to the pan and sauté for 5 minutes. Mix in the cabbage, carrots and peas. Place half this mixture in the base of a large casserole or cast-iron pot. Place the pheasant and half the drained prunes on top, then cover with the remaining cabbage mixture, remaining prunes and the wine. Arrange the smoked sausages on top. Bake at 180 °C, covered, for 2 hours, or cook in the cast-iron pot over the coals for about 2½–3 hours. Carve the pheasant, arrange the slices on a heated serving platter and arrange the prunes, cabbage mixture and sausages around it. Serve with Yellow Rice with Raisins (page 72).
Serves 4

VENISON POTJIE

Game was often cooked in a potjie over the fire for hours until tender and tasty. Any venison may be used to make this potjie; springbok is particularly good.

125 ml sunflower oil
4 medium carrots, sliced
2 medium onions, sliced
2 cloves garlic, crushed
10 ml chopped fresh thyme
1 kg venison, cubed
250 g rindless bacon, chopped

500 ml port or dry red wine
6 medium potatoes, sliced

Heat the oil in a cast-iron pot and sauté the carrots, onions and garlic for about 5 minutes. Add the thyme, meat, bacon and port or wine and simmer, covered, for 3 hours. Add the potatoes and simmer for a further 30–45 minutes. Serve with Mealie Porridge (page 74) or Crumbly Mealie Porridge (page 74).

Serves 8

POT-ROAST MUSCOVY DUCK

This was a favourite treat on Sundays or special occasions. The duck was pot-roasted in a heavy cast-iron pot over the fire – a long, slow method perfect for cooking it to succulent perfection. At the simmering stage, hot coals were heaped on the lid to ensure that the duck cooked evenly. The liver was fried separately in butter or fat and served with the duck.

1.5–2 kg Muscovy duck
1 clove garlic, halved
6 strips speck (pork fat) or
bacon rashers
10 ml salt
2 ml milled pepper
1 large onion, sliced
5 ml finely chopped fresh mixed herbs
50 ml butter or margarine
250 ml red wine

STUFFING
500 g pork sausage meat or pork mince
125 ml fresh white breadcrumbs
100 g rindless streaky bacon, chopped
10 ml chopped fresh parsley

1 large egg
2 ml finely chopped fresh mixed herbs
5 ml salt
2 ml milled pepper

First make the stuffing. Combine all the ingredients and set aside. Trim the Muscovy duck, and rub the carcass inside and out with the cut garlic clove. Fill the cavity with the stuffing and sew up the opening or secure it with skewers. Secure the strips of speck or bacon rashers to the breast and back of the duck and dust with salt and pepper. Place the duck in a saucepan with the sliced onion and sprinkle with the 5 ml mixed herbs. Add the butter or margarine and braise the duck, uncovered, for about 30 minutes, or until nicely browned, turning once or twice. Add the wine, cover and simmer over moderate to low heat for 2–2½ hours. Serve with Yellow Rice with Raisins (page 72) and lightly steamed vegetables.

Serves 4–6

VENISON LIVER IN CAUL FAT

Liver prepared this way is reminiscent of the Scottish haggis; indeed, the method is typical of many of the European 'puddings' prepared from offal.

1 kg venison liver, cleaned and
thickly sliced
5 ml salt
milled black pepper
caul fat

Season the venison liver and place it in the caul fat. Wrap it up and secure with skewer. Braai the liver over moderate coals for about 10–15 minutes, or until just done. Serve immediately with Crumbly Mealie Porridge (page 74).

Serves 6

VARIATION: The liver may also be minced with onion and a piece of white bread.

SADDLE OF SPRINGBOK WITH APRICOTS

Cooked this way, farm-reared springbok is meltingly tender and does not require a long cooking time.

60 ml Fruit Chutney (page 136)
3 kg saddle of springbok
2 cloves garlic, cut into slivers
125 g dried apricots, sliced
10 ml chopped fresh mixed herbs
15 ml salt
milled black pepper
250 g streaky bacon rashers

Spread the chutney over the meat. Make incisions next to the backbone and stuff with the garlic and apricots. Season with the herbs, salt and pepper. Place the bacon over the meat and roast, uncovered, at 180 °C for 40 minutes (see Note). Serve with Quince Jelly (page 130) or Baked Quinces (page 86).
Serves 8

NOTE: Overcooked meat becomes dry and tasteless.

Saddle of Springbok with Apricots and Baked Quinces (page 86).

GUINEAFOWL AND CHICKEN POTJIE

A mixture of wild and domestic birds makes this stew different and delicious.

1.5–2 kg young guineafowl
1.5 kg chicken
65 ml cake flour seasoned with 5 ml salt
and 2 ml milled pepper
125 ml sunflower oil
25 ml butter
250 g chopped bacon, preferably
green (unsmoked)
1 large onion, sliced
2 small carrots, chopped
1 stalk celery, chopped
2 cloves garlic, crushed
250 ml Chicken Stock (page 11)
500 ml dry red wine
2 sprigs of fresh parsley
2 bay or lemon leaves
1 sprig of fresh thyme
juice of 1 lemon
salt and milled black pepper

20 small onions
20 button mushrooms
20 small potatoes
2 stalks celery, coarsely chopped

Cut the guineafowl and chicken into portions. Coat the guineafowl pieces in the seasoned flour. Heat the oil and butter in a cast-iron pot. Brown the guineafowl for 5 minutes on each side. Add the bacon and sauté for 10 minutes. Add the onion, carrots, celery and garlic and cook, stirring, for 5 minutes. Add the stock, 250 ml of the wine, the parsley, bay or lemon leaves and thyme. Simmer, covered, for 40 minutes. Meanwhile, braai the chicken pieces quickly over the hot coals until browned, basting with oil and lemon juice during braaiing. Add to the pot and skim off the fat. Add the remaining wine and stir carefully. Adjust the seasoning, cover and simmer for a further 35 minutes. Add the onions, then layer the mushrooms, potatoes and celery on top. Simmer, covered, for approximately 1 hour.

Serves 8

VARIATION: Use 250 ml uncooked rice instead of the potatoes. Do not stir.

Guineafowl and Chicken Potjie, Braised Guineafowl and Game Bird Pie, three appetising ways with game birds.

BRAISED GUINEAFOWL

75 g butter or margarine
1.5–2 kg guineafowl, cut into portions
12 small onions
10 ml salt
2 ml milled pepper
5 ml chopped fresh mixed herbs
250 ml cream or natural yoghurt
15 ml paprika
juice of ½ lemon

Melt the butter or margarine in a large saucepan or casserole and brown the guineafowl pieces on all sides to seal in the juices. Add the onions to the saucepan and sauté for approximately 5 minutes, or until they are transparent. Add the salt, pepper and herbs, and braise the guineafowl, covered, for approximately 1–1½ hours, or until tender, adding a little water or chicken stock if the meat becomes too dry. Stir in the cream or yoghurt, paprika and lemon juice and serve on boiled browned rice, accompanied by stewed dried peaches or apricots.

Serves 6

GAME BIRD PIE

500 g Flaky Pastry (page 100)

FILLING
1 kg game bird flesh, boned
125 ml white wine
2–3 peppercorns
1 bay leaf
200 g rindless streaky bacon, chopped
15 ml chutney
125 g dried apricots, chopped
25 ml dry red wine
5 ml chopped fresh thyme
1 clove garlic, crushed

Halve the pastry and roll out one half. Line a pie dish and reserve the remaining pastry for the crust. To make the filling, stew the meat with the white wine, peppercorns and bay leaf for about 30 minutes. Add the remaining filling ingredients and spoon into the pie dish. Cover with the rolled-out reserved pastry, crimping the pastry edges together. Cut a few slits in the top to allow steam to escape during baking. Bake at 180 °C for 30 minutes, or until the pastry is golden. Serve with Yellow Rice with Raisins (page 72) and Quince Jelly (page 130).

Serves 8

POFADDER

This sausage has been made for generations in areas where game abounds. Any kind of game can be used, but springbok and kudu are particularly good.

large intestine of venison
venison liver, heart and kidneys, cleaned and diced
5 ml salt
milled pepper
30 ml crushed roasted coriander seeds
5 ml dried thyme
15 ml Worcestershire sauce

Clean the intestine thoroughly. Mix the liver, heart and kidneys with the salt, pepper, coriander seeds, thyme and the Worcestershire sauce, and stuff the mixture into the intestine. Braai over moderate coals for approximately 15–20 minutes, turning once. Serve, sliced, with Mealie Porridge (page 74).

Serves 6

VARIATIONS
• Use the small intestine to make a smaller sausage, called Skilpad.
• Use the intestine, liver, heart and kidneys of a sheep instead of venison.

CHAPTER 6

VEGETABLES, SALADS AND SIDE DISHES

The vegetables our great-grandparents cultivated and used most often were potatoes, sweet potatoes (soetpatats), carrots, onions and pumpkin. The cooking methods and the flavourings had varied origins. We are indebted to the Dutch for the addition of butter and grated nutmeg to vegetables like pumpkin, squash and marrows. The Malays added the sweet touch to vegetables. The Indians gave us rice coloured and flavoured with borrie (turmeric), while samp and mealies were staples for black people. What was served as a salad depended largely on where people lived. In the Cape, watercress, wild asparagus and cabbage, wild lettuce and the soft young shoots of the river palmiet (a bulrush), as well as the fleshy leaves of the vetkousie (a succulent) were gathered when fresh greens were required for a salad. Further inland, cooked salads were the order of the day.

BREADED PUMPKIN (PAMPOENMOES)

Pampoenmoes, a kind of vegetable pudding, is one of the oldest and most popular pumpkin recipes.

750 g peeled and sliced pumpkin
2 slices crustless white bread,
   buttered and cubed
5 ml salt
3 sticks cinnamon
30 ml butter
30 ml yellow or brown sugar
30 ml water

Layer the pumpkin and bread alternately in a greased ovenproof dish. Sprinkle with salt, add the cinnamon and dot with butter. Sprinkle with the sugar. Add the water and bake at 180 °C for 30 minutes, or until cooked and lightly browned. Serve with roast meat.
Serves 4

MICROWAVE OVEN: The pumpkin can first be par-cooked in the microwave oven. Peel and dice the pumpkin, place it in a microwave dish with 65 ml water and microwave at 100 per cent power for about 10 minutes.

VARIATION: Butternut squash can also be used to good effect in this recipe.

Breaded Pumpkin (top) and Pumpkin Fritters.

OVEN-BAKED PUMPKIN

The boer pumpkin (boerpampoen) is the best variety to use for this dish, although hubbard squash or butternut squash can also be prepared this way. Pumpkins grow extremely well in the drier interior of the country, and their great advantage is that they keep so well. In the past – and still today, in some areas – a traveller would see pumpkins stored on the flat tin roofs of houses and farm buildings.

1 kg pumpkin, sliced into segments
and peeled
Cinnamon Sugar (page 21) or sugar
mixed with ground ginger
60 ml water

Remove and reserve the pips from the pumpkin (see Pumpkin Pips, page 71). Arrange the pumpkin slices in an ovenproof dish and sprinkle with the cinnamon or ginger sugar. Add the water and bake at 180 °C for approximately 45 minutes.
Serves 6

PUMPKIN FRITTERS

These fritters, which are still a South African favourite, were served either as a vegetable or as a dessert.

500 ml cooked, drained and mashed pumpkin
1 large egg, beaten
30 ml cake flour
5 ml baking powder
1 ml salt
butter or sunflower oil
Cinnamon Sugar (page 21)
lemon slices

Combine the pumpkin, egg, flour, baking powder and salt. Heat the butter or oil in a frying pan and drop in spoonfuls of the pumpkin mixture. Fry the fritters for about 5 minutes on either side, or until golden. Serve hot, sprinkled with cinnamon sugar and garnished with lemon slices.

Serves 4

PUMPKIN PIPS (PAMPOENPITTE)

Nutritious pumpkin pips served as a snack are popular in this country. The Sotho people like them fried, Portuguese people like them baked (dry-roasted), and they were important as a nutritive source to the early settlers in many parts of our country. In years gone by, you could buy them at street markets– the Grand Parade in Cape Town, for instance – but they are not as freely available today. To make your own, bake cleaned pumpkin pips at 150 °C until dry. Sprinkle with salt and serve as a snack with drinks.

FRIED GREEN MEALIES

Traditionally mealies cut from the cob were cooked this way, but this updated version uses the currently fashionable very young mealies.

12 whole baby mealies
sunflower oil
salt
chopped fresh chives

Fry the mealies (allow 3 per person) in a little sunflower oil until golden, shaking the pan occasionally. Sprinkle with salt and chives and serve.

Serves 4

STEWED SWEET POTATOES (GESTOOFDE SOETPATATS)

Naartjie peel adds a distinctive and traditional South African flavour to these sweet potatoes.

1.5 kg sweet potatoes, sliced
100 g butter
200 ml water
3 pieces Dried Naartjie Peel (page 97)
2 sticks cinnamon or 1 piece root ginger, crushed
5 ml salt
250 g brown sugar
30 ml honey

Place all the ingredients in a heavy-based saucepan. Stew over moderate heat until all the water has evaporated, shaking the saucepan occasionally to prevent sticking and burning. Remove the naartjie peel and cinnamon sticks or ginger before serving.

Serves 6

MICROWAVE OVEN: Place all the ingredients in a glass or microwave dish and microwave at 100 per cent power for 2–4 minutes.

NOTE: Small yellow-skinned borrie patats are the best variety to use, but if they are unavailable, white wurgpatats may also be used.

YELLOW RICE WITH RAISINS (GEELRYS)

Despite repeated efforts to grow rice at the Cape, Jan van Riebeeck had to admit defeat. This did not sit well with the Here Sewentien in Holland; rice was a staple food for the slaves who worked in the colony, which meant that it had to be imported. Another name for yellow rice was funeral rice (begrafnisrys) because – in both the Malay and Dutch communities – it was always served at the meals held after funerals, a custom which persists today. The practice of colouring rice with turmeric (borrie) was introduced to this country by Indian immigrants.

250 ml uncooked white rice
10 ml turmeric
1 stick cinnamon
5 ml salt
30 ml yellow sugar
125 ml seedless raisins or sultanas
10 ml butter

Place the rice, turmeric, cinnamon, salt and sugar in a saucepan. Cover with water and boil for about 15–20 minutes, or until the rice is tender and all the moisture has been absorbed. Add the raisins or sultanas and steam the mixture in a colander over a saucepan of boiling water for 30 minutes. Remove the cinnamon stick, fluff the rice with the butter and serve with curries or Bobotie (page 45).

Serves 6

SALTED GREEN BEANS

In the past, preserving fruit and vegetables for use in winter when fresh produce was not available was an important task of every housewife. Beans were sliced and layered in an earthenware or stone jar alternately with coarse salt. When needed, they were washed well to remove as much salt as possible and used in dishes like Bean Bredie (page 51).

WATERBLOMMETJIE STEW

Waterblommetjies, found along the waterways of the Cape Peninsula and Boland, are uniquely South African. Widely used in the 17th and 18th centuries, waterblommetjies are once again popular.

500 g waterblommetjies, trimmed and washed well
1 potato, sliced
1 onion, sliced
5 ml salt
2 ml milled white pepper
100 ml water

sorrel to taste, 1 grated tart green apple or 5 ml lemon juice for flavouring

Place the waterblommetjies, potato, onion, salt and pepper in a saucepan. Add the water and simmer for approximately 30–40 minutes, or until tender but still crisp. Add the sorrel, apple or lemon juice and serve the stew with cooked rice.

Serves 6

GREEN BEANS IN EGG SAUCE

A traditional salad in which the crispness of green beans combines perfectly with the piquant sweet-sour taste of an egg and vinegar sauce. This subtle blending of flavours is typical of boerekos.

500 g whole young green beans, topped and tailed

2 ml milled white pepper
1 large egg, beaten

SAUCE
60 ml water
30 ml brown vinegar
15 ml sugar
2 ml salt

Cook the beans in boiling salted water for about 15 minutes, or until just tender. Drain and leave to cool. To make the sauce, beat together the water, vinegar, sugar, salt and pepper. Add the egg, still beating. Place the bowl over boiling water and beat until it thickens. Pour over the beans and serve.

Serves 6

GREEN BEAN AND POTATO STEW

This dish is a typical example of the hearty, homely fare Afrikaners refer to as boerekos.

500 g green beans, topped and tailed
1 potato, sliced
1 onion, sliced
5 ml salt
2 ml milled white pepper
100 ml water
2 ml freshly grated nutmeg

Slice the beans into a saucepan. Add the potato, onion, salt and pepper. Add the water and simmer the mixture, covered, for 30–40 minutes, or until cooked.

Sprinkle with the grated nutmeg and serve as an accompaniment to meat dishes.
Serves 6–8

MICROWAVE OVEN: Par-cook the beans in a glass dish with 50 ml water and a little salt. Cover with vented plastic and microwave at 100 per cent power for 10–12 minutes, or until tender.

VARIATIONS
- Use 500 g grated cabbage instead of the beans and add 5 ml lemon juice or a grated tart green apple.
- Use 500 g chopped spinach instead of beans. Omit the water and add a little sorrel for flavouring.

VEGETABLE CURRY

The hot vegetable curries of India and other parts of the East get the subtle and aromatic Cape treatment with the addition of dried peaches.

50 ml sunflower oil
1 piece root ginger, minced
2 cloves garlic, crushed
1 medium onion, sliced
7 ml turmeric
5 ml salt
10 ml curry powder
125 ml water
750 g sliced mixed carrots, beans, cauliflower and green sweet pepper
200 g waterblommetjies
200 g peeled dried peaches, soaked overnight in water and drained

Heat the oil in a saucepan and sauté the ginger and garlic briefly. Add the onion and sauté for about 5 minutes, or until transparent. Stir in the turmeric, salt and curry powder, then add the water, mixed vegetables, waterblommetjies and peaches, and simmer for 20 minutes. Serve on cooked brown rice with desiccated coconut and Fruit Chutney (page 136).
Serves 6

Vegetable Curry, Green Bean and Potato Stew and Yellow Rice with Rraisins.

MEALIE PORRIDGE (STYWEPAP, PUTUPAP)

Mealie meal, from which this porridge is made, is the staple food of many South Africans. The porridge is a firm favourite as a braai accompaniment.

10 ml salt
750 ml to 1 litre boiling water
500 ml unsifted mealie meal
125 ml cold water

Add the salt to the boiling water, then add the mealie meal to the centre of the saucepan, without stirring. Cover and simmer for 45 minutes to 1 hour. Stir with a fork or wooden spoon, add the cold water and simmer for a further hour. Serve with tomato and onion sauce or gravy.
Serves 6

CRUMBLY MEALIE PORRIDGE (KRUMMELPAP)

This crumbly mealie porridge is a staple for many people in South Africa, and as popular a braai accompaniment as stywepap.

250 ml water
5 ml salt
500 ml coarse yellow mealie meal

Boil the water and salt. Sprinkle the mealie meal over the water and boil for 15 minutes. Stir the porridge with a fork or wooden spoon to obtain a crumbly consistency and then simmer, partially covered, for 30 minutes.
Serves 6

Purslane (posteleinblaar)
The leaves of the herb purslane were a popular flavouring in the past, but they were also braised with ginger, mace, pepper and wine and served with rice and potatoes.

Mealie Porridge (top) and Crumbly Mealie Porridge, staple foods for many South Africans.

Oils for cold sauces
Just about the only cold sauce (or dressing) made in the early days of the Dutch settlement at the Cape was sour sauce, made by beating together egg, vinegar, salt and pepper. The reason for this was that there was a scarcity of locally pressed vegetable oils. Coconut oil and the various seed oils were imported from the East, but were expensive. Some alternative had to be found, so the colonists started extracting the oil for sauce-making of all kinds from fats. One of the most widely used methods was to skim the oil from the surface of the first boiling of trotters or meat containing tendons or fat. This was clarified, bottled and used to make salad dressings.

BAKED SWEET POTATOES (GEBAKTE PATATS)

This is one of the simplest traditional ways to prepare sweet potatoes, which was used to make either yellow borrie patats or the larger white sweet potatoes which are called wurgpatats.

6–12 small yellow sweet potatoes (borrie patats)
sunflower oil or butter

Wash the unpeeled sweet potatoes well and pat them dry. Rub them with sunflower oil or butter and place them on a baking sheet. Bake at 150 °C for 1½–2 hours, or until soft. Test with a skewer, or press the sweet potatoes lightly: they are done if the flesh gives slightly. Serve with butter.
Serves 6

NOTE: Braaied Whole Snoek (page 25) is difficult to imagine without the traditional accompaniments of these baked sweet potatoes, wholewheat bread and korrelkonfyt (see Grape Jam, page 130).

SAMP AND BEANS

Mealies and beans were (and still are) staple foods in Africa, and this dish is basic to many daily diets.

125 g dried beans, soaked overnight in water
125 g samp, soaked overnight in water
1.5 litres boiling water
salt to taste

Drain the beans and samp and add to the boiling water. Cook over moderate heat for about 3 hours, adding water and salt when necessary to obtain a soft but not watery consistency.
Serves 4

SOUSBOONTJIES

This traditional bean salad is still as popular as ever. In the past, it was a way of preserving beans.

200 g dried sugar beans
30 ml butter
30 ml sugar
30 ml water
60 ml brown vinegar
2 ml salt

Soak the beans overnight in cold water to cover. Drain, cover with fresh water in a saucepan and cook for about 30 minutes, or until tender. Drain, add the remaining ingredients and simmer for 10 minutes. Serve hot as a vegetable, or cold as a salad. The beans can also be packed into jars, sealed, sterilized and stored. Store in the refrigerator once opened.
Serves 6

WATERCRESS SALAD

Watercress was gathered along the waterways of the Cape Peninsula and the Boland and used as a garnish, as well as for this salad.

1 bunch watercress

DRESSING
1 hard-boiled egg yolk, mashed
100 ml brown vinegar
50 ml sunflower oil
2 ml mustard powder
2 ml salt

Wash the watercress and remove the stalks. Place the leaves in a salad bowl. Thoroughly combine all the ingredients for the dressing and pour over the watercress just before serving.
Serves 6

ONION SALAD (SLAPHAKSKEENTJIES)

This salad is another example of the combination of sweet and sour flavours.

1 kg unpeeled pickling onions

SAUCE
5 ml salt
10 ml mustard powder
15 ml cornflour
125 ml sugar
3 large eggs, beaten well
125 ml brown vinegar
200 ml milk
250 ml cream

Boil the onions in boiling salted water for 15 minutes, or until just tender. Drain, leave to cool, then remove the skins. To make the sauce, combine the salt, mustard powder, cornflour and sugar in a bowl. Add the eggs and beat until creamy. Add the vinegar, beating constantly. Combine the milk and cream and beat it into the mustard mixture. Heat over low heat and simmer, stirring constantly, until the mixture thickens. Remove from the stove immediately, pour over the onions and leave to cool.

Serves 8

GLAZED BEETROOT SALAD

My mother always served cucumber salad with Bean Bredie (page 51) and this beetroot salad with curries.

12 young beetroot
30 ml butter
2 small onions, sliced
6 pickling onions, chopped
15 ml honey
15 ml cake flour
5 ml brown vinegar
5 ml salt
5 ml chopped fresh marjoram

Scrape and quarter the beetroot. Melt the butter and sauté the onions for about 5 minutes until transparent. Add the beetroot and simmer for 5 minutes, adding a little water if necessary. Combine the honey, flour and vinegar and add to the beetroot and onions. Add the salt and marjoram and simmer, covered, for 20 minutes. Serve hot as a vegetable or cold as a salad.

Serves 6

QUINCE SAMBAL

Quinces, which grow extremely well throughout the country, have a piquant taste that goes particularly well with curry dishes.

1 quince
2 ml salt
1 small onion, grated
1 small red chilli, finely chopped
30 ml white sugar

Peel and grate the quince. Sprinkle with the salt, then mix well with the other ingredients.

Makes about 250 ml

LOQUAT SAMBAL

These small, slightly tart fruits were once a feature of almost every garden.

1 kg loquats, peeled and stoned
1 onion, chopped
2 drops Tabasco® sauce
2 ml salt

Combine all the ingredients well.

Makes about 250 ml

CARROT SAMBAL

4–6 young carrots
2 ml salt
2 ml freshly grated nutmeg
1 ml milled white pepper
10 ml brown vinegar or lemon juice

Grate the carrots and mix with the remaining ingredients until well blended.
Makes about 250 ml

CUCUMBER SAMBAL

Cucumber sambal is a traditional accompaniment to Bean Bredie (page 51) as well as curries.

1 large cucmber, peeled and
coarsely grated
30 ml brown vinegar
5 ml finely chopped fresh dill

5 ml salt
2 ml milled white pepper

Combine all the ingredients well.
Makes about 250 ml

APPLE SAMBAL

This sambal is delicious with curries.

1 tart green apple
2 ml salt
1 small onion, grated
1 small chilli, seeded and finely chopped
30 ml white sugar ʒT

Peel and grate the apple and sprinkle with the salt. Mix with the remaining ingredients.
Makes about 250 ml

Sambals
The Indians and Malays have been making sambals – chunky, fresh relishes usually served with curries – for centuries. Many sambals are spicy, if not decidedly hot, with the addition of chillies. Most of them will keep for a day or two in the refrigerator, but are best used immediately.

Clockwise from the top: Quince Sambal, Cucumber Sambal, Onion Salad, Carrot Sambal, Glazed Beetroot Salad and Apple Sambal. Sambals are usually served with curries.

CHAPTER 7

DESSERTS

Fresh fruit was always a popluar offering at the end of the meal in the early days of settlement, and there was always salt, pepper, ground ginger and cinnamon on the table to sprinkle over the fruit. Oranges, strawberries, peaches and melons were generally served with salt and, although we do not often serve fruit this way today, the habit persists in some communities. Fruit like oranges were also often sprinkled with salt and then baked. Among the first cold puddings to be introduced were Blancmange (page 81) and Lemon Snow or sneeupoeding (page 80). Gelatine was unknown, and up to the early decades of this century, isinglass or seaweed (kelp jelly) was used to set cold desserts. Hot puddings were brought to this country by the Huguenots and the British settlers. Ginger and cinnamon were popular flavourings, as were lemon and orange rind and Dried Naartjie Peel (page 97), and peach leaves were used to obtain an almond flavour.

LEMON SNOW

This delectable, melt-in-the-mouth fruit dessert is delightfully refreshing on a hot day.

15 ml gelatine
65 ml cold water
250 ml hot water
65 ml lemon juice
grated rind of ½ lemon
200 g white sugar
2 large egg whites

Sprinkle the gelatine over the cold water and leave it to soak for 15 minutes, or until spongy. Add the hot water and stir to dissolve the gelatine. Stir in the lemon juice and rind and the sugar. Leave the jelly to cool until the mixture starts to set. Whisk the egg whites until stiff peaks form. Beat the lemon mixture with a rotary beater until foamy, then fold in the egg whites. Pour the mixture into a mould rinsed with cold water or sprayed with non-stick cooking spray and chill in the refrigerator until set. Serve with chilled custard or lemon sauce.
Serves 4

WINE JELLY

It was the custom to serve this wine jelly, spooned into special jelly glasses, along with home-made preserves when coffee and tea were offered at the end of a birthday celebration.

30 ml gelatine
60 ml cold water
300 ml boiling water
75 ml white sugar
5 whole cloves
2 sticks cinnamon
250 ml port
5 ml lemon essence

Sprinkle the gelatine over the cold water and leave to soak for about 15 minutes, or until spongy. Place the boiling water, sugar, cloves and cinnamon in a small saucepan and simmer the mixture over low heat for 5 minutes. Add the gelatine and stir until it dissolves. Allow the mixture to cool slightly, then stir in the port and lemon essence. Allow to set at room temperature (the jelly must be fairly soft). Break up the jelly, removing the cloves and cinnamon, and spoon into jelly glasses or dessert bowls. Serve with custard if desired.
Serves 6–8

Clockwise from top left: Wine Jelly, Blancmange and Trifle, time-honoured treats for dessert.

TRIFLE

Christmas wouldn't be Christmas without a trifle. The 18th century European original was a rich affair composed of cake or biscuits soaked in wine or sherry, topped with custard or syllabub and decorated with almonds, ratafia biscuits and crystallized fruits and flowers. Nearly every modern cook has her own trifle recipe (very often a family recipe handed down through the generations), but all of them contain sponge cake, custard, jelly, fruit and cream. Start making the trifle the day before, to allow time for the individual layers to set.

8–10 slices Sponge Cake (page 96) or a bought sponge loaf, sliced
125–190 ml sweet sherry, red muscadel or port
100 g mixed nuts, coarsely chopped
2 x 80 g packets port wine (or blackberry) jelly powder
450 ml boiling water
2 x 410 g cans youngberries, drained (see Note)
2–3 pieces preserved ginger or Watermelon Preserve (page 122), chopped
about 2 cups home-made custard
250 ml cream, whipped
glacé cherries, preserved ginger (or watermelon) and angelica

Arrange the slices of cake in a large, deep, glass bowl. Drizzle the sherry, muscadel or port over the cake. Sprinkle the nuts on top. Dissolve the jelly powder in the boiling water and pour it carefully over the nuts. Allow it to cool slightly, then chill in the refrigerator until the jelly has set. Arrange the youngberries and preserved ginger or watermelon on top of the jelly. Make the custard and pour it over the fruit. Chill in the refrigerator until the custard has set. Just before serving, spread the whipped cream on top and decorate with cherries, ginger or watermelon and angelica.

Serves 6–8

NOTE: The juice from the youngberries makes a refreshing drink, diluted with soda water.

BLANCMANGE (BLAMAANS)

Blancmange – or cornflour mould, as it was often called in the domestic science textbooks of the 1930s – was one of the first puddings developed in medieval Europe. The recipe probably made its way here via the Dutch or French. Our great-grandmothers poured the mixture into a copper mould and stood it in a dish of cold water to aid setting. Sometimes the blancmange was coloured pink (by adding a drop or two of cochineal) and sometimes the eggs were separated and the whites beaten into one half of the mixture and the yolks beaten into the other so that, when set, the blancmange had two layers.

250 ml cornflour
2 ml salt
120 g white sugar
1.5 litres milk
3 peach leaves or 7 ml almond essence
2 large eggs, beaten

Combine the cornflour, salt and sugar. Add 100 ml of the milk and mix to a smooth paste. Place the rest of the milk in a saucepan, add the peach leaves and bring to the boil. (If you are using almond essence, add it after the eggs.) Remove the peach leaves when the milk has boiled. Stir in the cornflour mixture and continue cooking, stirring constantly, until thick. Simmer for approximately 3 minutes to cook through. Remove the saucepan from the stove, stir in the eggs and then the almond essence, if using. Pour the mixture into a mould which has been rinsed with cold water or sprayed with non-stick cooking spray, and allow to set, either at room temperature or in the refrigerator. Turn out onto a serving platter and serve with the syrup from the Green Fig Preserve (page 123) or Watermelon Preserve (page 122).

Serves 4–6

SPONGING GELATINE IN THE MICROWAVE OVEN

Measure the required quantity of liquid into a microwave jug or bowl. Sprinkle the gelatine over and leave to stand for a few minutes. Microwave at 50 per cent power until dissolved. As a general rule, 45 seconds to 1 minute's microwaving time is required for 45–90 ml liquid.

CAPE BRANDY PUDDING

Brandy has a long history in South Africa, from the earliest distillation of Cape grapes — believed to be in 1672 and rightfully termed 'fire water' — to the refined product available today.

250 g dates, stoned and finely chopped
5 ml bicarbonate of soda
250 ml boiling water
125 g butter or margarine
200 g white sugar
2 large eggs, beaten
240 g cake flour
5 ml baking powder
2 ml salt
250 ml finely chopped walnuts or pecan nuts

SYRUP
15 ml butter or margarine
200 g white sugar
150 ml water
125 ml brandy
5 ml vanilla essence
1 ml salt

Mix half of the dates with the bicarbonate of soda and pour the boiling water over the dates. Mix well and leave to cool. Cream the butter or margarine and sugar together until light, then beat in the eggs to make a smooth mixture. Sift the flour, baking powder and salt over the creamed mixture and fold it in. Mix in the remaining dates and the nuts. Stir in the bicarbonate of soda and date mixture, mix well and turn the batter into a large baking dish. Bake at 180 °C for approximately 40 minutes, or until the pudding springs back when pressed in the centre. Make the syrup just before the pudding is cooked. Heat the butter or margarine, sugar and water for approximately 5 minutes, remove the mixture from the stove and stir in the brandy, vanilla essence and salt. Pour the warm syrup over the pudding as soon as it comes from the oven. Serve the pudding either hot or cold, with whipped cream.

Serves 6

MICROWAVE OVEN: Microwave the pudding at 70 per cent power for 13–15 minutes. Leave to stand for 10 minutes. Microwave the syrup at 70 per cent power for 2–3 minutes, stirring once. Pour the syrup over the pudding and serve.

CHRISTMAS PUDDING

Christmas pudding is an extremely important part of the festive meal in South Africa. Make your pudding well in advance – about a month – as it needs time to mature. Store it in a dry, well-ventilated place until needed, and steam it again before serving. The old custom was to put silver (or silver coloured) coins in the pudding for the children to scrabble over when eating the pudding. But what about the new South African coins that are not even silver coloured? Do what the British did with the old wooden thruppenny bit: wrap the coins in waxed paper or – more authentic-looking – in aluminium foil before inserting them in the pudding. And, if you are making or reheating the pudding in the microwave oven, press the coins into the pudding just before serving.

450 g fruit cake mix
200 g white sugar
250 ml water
90 ml butter or margarine
5 ml salt
5 ml ground mixed spice
125 ml chopped glacé cherries
125 ml chopped preserved ginger
5 ml bicarbonate of soda
500 ml cake flour
5 ml baking powder
250 ml chopped mixed nuts
2 large eggs, beaten

Combine the fruit cake mix, sugar, water, butter or margarine, salt, mixed spice, cherries and ginger. Bring to the boil and boil for 5 minutes. Allow to cool. Stir in the bicarbonate of soda. Sift the flour and baking powder, then stir into the cooled fruit mixture. Stir in the nuts and the beaten eggs, and mix well. Pour the batter into a greased pudding basin. Cover the basin with a double layer of waxed paper and tie securely with string. Place the basin in a large saucepan half filled with water and steam, covered, for 1¼ hours, or steam in a pressure cooker for about 45 minutes. Remove from the saucepan and allow to cool. Store until needed. To serve, steam the pudding again for about 1 hour, then turn the pudding out onto a serving plate. If desired, pour heated brandy over and flame it. Serve the pudding with Brandy Sauce (page 86) or custard.

Serves 8–10

MICROWAVE OVEN: Microwave the pudding, covered with vented plastic, at 50 per cent power for approximately 20–25 minutes. Reheat at 50 per cent power for 10 minutes. Leave to stand for 3–4 minutes.

BAKED LEMON PUDDING

As it bakes, this pudding separates into a layer of sponge over a base of tangy lemon curd.

125 g white sugar
50 ml butter
15 ml boiling water
50 g cake flour
juice and grated rind of 1 large lemon
2 large eggs, separated
225 ml milk

Beat the sugar and butter until creamy, then beat in the boiling water. Stir in the flour, lemon juice and lemon rind. Beat the egg yolks and milk together. Add to the creamed mixture, a little at a time, beating well after each addition. Whisk the egg whites until stiff and fold them into the pudding mixture. Pour the mixture into a greased ovenproof dish and place it in a roasting pan half filled with hot water. Bake at 170 °C for 45 minutes. Serve hot, or cool slightly and serve with pouring cream.
Serves 4–6

JAM ROLY-POLY

From the top left: Christmas Pudding, Brandy Sauce (page 86) and Cape Brandy Pudding.

Introduced by the British, this dessert was adopted with great enthusiasm in South Africa.

240 g cake flour
10 ml baking powder
2 ml salt
100 ml butter or margarine
2 large eggs
60 ml milk or iced water
smooth apricot jam
750 ml boiling water
400 g white sugar
10 ml vanilla or lemon essence

Sift the flour, baking powder and salt together. Cut in 60 ml of the butter or margarine with a knife. Beat the eggs and the milk or iced water together and mix with the flour mixture to make a stiff dough. Roll the dough into a rectangle on a floured board and spread apricot jam over it. Roll it up and place the roll, seam-side down, in a greased baking dish. Combine the remaining butter or margarine, boiling water, sugar and vanilla or lemon essence and pour over the roll. Bake at 180 °C for 1 hour. Serve the roll slightly cooled with custard.
Serves 6–8

BUTTERMILK PUDDING (KARRINGMELKPOEDING)

There was always buttermilk (the liquid remaining when butter is churned) available on the farm, and it was used in all sorts of dishes, as a marinade for meat and also in this pudding. Cultured buttermilk is available commercially nowadays, so this old-fashioned pudding is as popular as ever.

50 ml butter or margarine
200 g white sugar
4 large eggs
240 g cake flour
2 ml salt
500 ml buttermilk
10 ml baking powder
5 ml grated lemon rind

Cream the butter or margarine and sugar together until creamy. Beat in the eggs to make a smooth mixture. Sift the flour and salt together, then stir it into the creamed mixture alternately with the buttermilk. Stir in the baking powder and the lemon rind. Pour the batter into a greased, oven-proof dish and bake it at 180 °C for 30–35 minutes, or until puffed up and lightly browned. Serve the pudding immediately with moskonfyt (see Grape Must Jam, page 127), or Orange Preserve (page 123).
Serves 4–6

From the top: Buttermilk Pudding, Orange Preserve (page 123) and Stuffed Baked Apples.

VINEGAR PUDDING (ASYNPOEDING)

Our ancestors viewed this delicious pudding as a standby recipe, ideal to prepare in a jiffy if guests arrived unexpectedly, because it used ingredients that every housewife would have in her pantry.

SYRUP
500 ml water
400 g white sugar
125 ml brown vinegar

2 ml freshly grated nutmeg
2 ml salt
30 ml smooth apricot jam

PUDDING
30 ml butter
125 ml brown sugar
2 large eggs, beaten
180 g cake flour
5 ml bicarbonate of soda
10 ml ground ginger

First make the syrup. Boil the water, sugar and vinegar for 5 minutes, then set aside to cool. To make the pudding, cream the butter and brown sugar together, then add the eggs, beating constantly. Sift the flour, bicarbonate of soda, ginger, nutmeg and salt into the egg mixture and mix well. Blend in the jam. Pour the cooled syrup into a baking or ovenproof dish, and spoon in the batter. Bake the pudding at 180 °C for 40 minutes. Serve warm with custard.
Serves 6

STUFFED BAKED APPLES

This recipe has been passed down from generation to generation in my mother's family and, although based on the standard dessert that's made in many parts of the world, it's the fruit and brandy filling that makes this version particularly South African.

6 large tart green apples, cored
200 ml sweet dessert wine

FILLING
6 large dried apricot halves, chopped
30 ml brandy
20 ml soft brown sugar
15 ml chopped currants

Make a shallow cut around the middle of each apple to prevent bursting during cooking. To make the filling, soak the apricots in the brandy for about 3 hours, or until plump. Mix the apricots and brandy with the brown sugar and chopped currants. Divide the mixture into 6 portions and use to fill the hollows in the apples. Place the apples in a baking dish and pour the wine over them. Cover the dish lightly with foil and bake at 180 °C for about 45 minutes, or until the apples are tender, basting occasionally with the wine. Place the apples on serving plates, drizzle a little of the wine sauce over them and serve immediately with whipped cream or custard.
Serves 6

MICROWAVE OVEN: Cut off a 2 cm-wide strip of skin from the top of each apple. Pierce the apples in a number of places, using a skewer, to prevent bursting during cooking. Prepare the filling and stuff the apples. Place them in a large dish and pour the wine over. Microwave at 70 per cent power for about 15 minutes, or until tender, basting from time to time with the pan juices. Allow the apples to stand for 5 minutes, then serve.

STEAMED GINGER PUDDING

Steamed puddings, probably introduced to South Africa by the British, have been winter-time favourites for many years in this country.

100 ml castor sugar
85 ml butter or margarine
2 large eggs, lightly beaten
110 g self-raising flour
5 ml ground ginger
60 g preserved ginger, diced
15 ml milk

Cream the sugar and butter or margarine until soft and light. Add the beaten eggs gradually, stirring constantly. Sift the flour and ginger into the bowl and stir into the mixture. Mix in the preserved ginger. Stir in the milk and pour the batter into a greased pudding basin. Cover the basin with a double layer of waxed paper or clean muslin, tie with string and steam in a large saucepan half filled with boiling water for about 1½ hours, or steam in a pressure cooker for about 45 minutes. Turn the pudding out onto a heated serving plate and serve immediately with a ginger sauce or any other sweet sauce.
Serves 4–6

VARIATION: To make a plain steamed pudding, leave out the ginger and use 5 ml vanilla essence instead. Serve with a sweet sauce of your choice.

MICROWAVE OVEN: Pour the batter into a large bowl, cover with vented plastic and microwave at 100 per cent power for 15 minutes. Allow to stand for 10 minutes before serving.

BAKED QUINCES

Quinces were once favourites for family desserts in all parts of the country. Nearly every farm had a quince tree or two in the garden, and the old-fashioned fruits were baked, puréed, bottled and made into jams and chutneys. Quinces take rather a long time to become tender if they are baked whole, but the cooking time is considerably reduced if they are sliced first. Honey — the main means of sweetening desserts in the past — combines piquantly with the flavour of the quinces, and the pink colour is obtained by leaving the pips in the fruit during cooking.

3 ripe quinces, peeled and sliced
125 ml honey
125 ml water
2 sticks cinnamon
50 ml butter or margarine

Arrange the quinces in overlapping rows in a greased, ovenproof dish. Drizzle the honey over the quince slices, then pour the water over them.

Add the cinnamon sticks. Dot with the butter or margarine and bake, covered lightly with foil, at 180 °C for about 40 minutes. Remove the foil and baste the quince slices with the pan juices. Test the quince slices; if they are tender but not mushy, serve immediately with custard. If they are still slightly hard, bake for a further 10–15 minutes
Serves 4

MICROWAVE OVEN: Assemble the dish and microwave, uncovered, at 50 per cent power for 10–15 minutes, or until tender but not mushy. Allow to stand for 5 minutes before serving.

RICE PUDDING

There are quite a number of traditional ways to make rice pudding, perhaps the best-known being the baked one introduced to South Africa by the British. Portugal, too, has its own version of rice pudding: the rice is boiled in water flavoured with salt and lemon rind before being simmered, over low heat, in milk to which a liberal 12 egg yolks have been added.

500 ml milk
250 ml cooked, long-grain rice (see Note)
2 large eggs, separated
125 ml white sugar
1 ml salt
2 ml vanilla essence

Heat the milk to lukewarm and stir in the rice. Remove from the stove.

Beat the egg yolks with the sugar and salt, then gradually add the milk mixture, beating constantly. Whisk the egg whites until stiff and fold into the rice mixture. Stir in the vanilla essence and pour the mixture into a greased, ovenproof dish. Bake the pudding at 180 °C for about 40 minutes, or until set. Serve the pudding hot with golden syrup, honey, or the syrup from Green Fig Preserve (page 123) or Watermelon Preserve (page 122).
Serves 4

NOTE: Leftover cooked rice was often used to make this dessert.

BRANDY SAUCE

This sauce is traditionally served with Christmas Pudding (page 82).

250 ml thick cream
15 ml brandy
30 g soft brown sugar
1 egg white

Whip the cream until it starts to thicken, then add the brandy and sugar and whip the cream until thick. Whisk the egg white until stiff but not dry. Using a metal spoon, fold the egg white into the cream mixture. Turn the sauce into a serving dish and serve.
Serves 4–6

MARSHMALLOW PUDDING (MALVAPOEDING)

This rich pudding contains no marshmallows, but probably got its name from its spongy texture.

250 ml castor sugar
2 large eggs
15 ml smooth apricot jam
185 g cake flour
5 ml bicarbonate of soda
pinch of salt
30 ml butter or margarine
5 ml white vinegar
125 ml milk

SAUCE
250 ml cream
125 ml butter
125 ml white sugar
125 ml water, orange juice or sherry

Beat the castor sugar and eggs until fluffy and light. Beat in the apricot jam. Sift the flour, bicarbonate of soda and salt together 3 times. Melt the butter or margarine with the vinegar and milk over low heat. Fold the flour mixture and the milk mixture alternately into the egg mixture and pour the batter into a greased ovenproof dish. Bake the pudding at 180 °C for about 45 minutes, or until a knife inserted in the centre comes out clean. Place all the ingredients for the sauce into a saucepan and stir over moderate heat until the butter has melted and the sugar has dissolved. Do not allow the mixture to boil. Remove the pudding from the oven, pierce it in a number of places with a skewer and pour the hot sauce over it immediately. Serve hot or cold, with cream.
Serves 10

From the top: Marshmallow Pudding, Rice Pudding and Baked Quinces.

BREAD AND BUTTER PUDDING

Thrifty British housewives discovered that this pudding was a delicious way to use up stale bread, and South Africans soon followed their example. Currants were originally used, but seedless raisins are just as good. Use a smaller quantity of raisins, however, otherwise they tend to overpower the flavour and spoil the appearance of the pudding.

4 slices stale white bread, 2 cm thick
butter
190 ml currants or 150 ml seedless raisins
2 large eggs
125 ml white sugar
1 ml salt
750 ml milk

Remove the crusts from the bread. Butter the slices thickly and place them, buttered sides down, in a greased, ovenproof dish. Sprinkle the currants or raisins over the bread. Beat the eggs well, then stir in the sugar, salt and milk. Pour the milk and egg mixture over the bread and set the dish aside for 30 minutes to allow the liquid to soak right through the bread. Bake the pudding, covered, at 160 °C for 30 minutes. Uncover the pudding and bake it for a further 10–15 minutes, or until the top is golden. Serve the pudding hot with golden syrup, honey or moskonfyt (see Grape Must Jam, page 127).
Serves 4–6

From the top: Bread and Butter Pudding and Traditional Pancakes.

TRADITIONAL PANCAKES (PANNEKOEK)

Go to a fête or bazaar anywhere in South Africa and you will find someone making and selling pancakes served with Cinnamon Sugar (page 21). Pancakes have been a tradition in this country from the earliest days of settlement, when they were made with special long-handled irons over the open fire, and served with honey and cream or, sometimes, with Van der Hum Liqueur (page 142).

240 g cake flour
2 ml baking powder
2 ml salt
2 large eggs
600 ml milk
60 ml cream
30 ml melted butter or sunflower oil
15 ml brandy
sunflower oil

Combine the cake flour, baking powder and salt. Beat the eggs and milk until foamy, then gradually beat in the flour mixture. Beat in the cream, then the melted butter or oil and the brandy. Heat a small frying pan and grease it lightly with oil. Pour in a thin layer of the pancake batter, tilting the pan to distribute it evenly. Fry the pancake on one side for about 1 minute, or until lightly browned, then turn the pancake with a spatula and fry it for another minute. Turn the pancake out onto a plate and keep warm while making the remaining pancakes. Roll up the pancakes and serve them with Cinnamon Sugar (page 21) and lemon wedges.

Serves 6

NOTE: Pancakes freeze very well. Interleave them with plastic and then overwrap them before freezing. To use, thaw the pancakes at room temperature and then reheat them on a plate over a saucepan of simmering water.

CINNAMON DUMPLINGS (SOUSKLUITJIES)

The tradition of making dumplings was introduced by Dutch settlers in South Africa, and this dessert has been around for almost as long. Nothing beats the taste of hot cinnamon dumplings eaten in front of an open fire on a cold winter evening.

120 g cake flour
5 ml baking powder
1 ml salt
60 ml butter
2 large eggs
15 ml white sugar
500 ml water
pinch of salt
butter
Cinnamon Sugar (page 21)

Sift the flour, baking powder and salt together. Rub in the butter. Beat the eggs and sugar together until light and mix with the flour mixture to make a thick batter. Bring the water and salt to the boil in a large, shallow saucepan with a tight-fitting lid. Dip a teaspoon into the boiling water to heat it, then scoop up a spoonful of batter and drop it into the boiling water. Repeat, first dipping the spoon into the water each time, until all the batter has been used. (Take care, however, not to cook too many dumplings at once – they should not touch one another.) Cover the saucepan and simmer the dumplings over low heat for about 10–15 minutes. Remove the dumplings with a slotted spoon and place them in a warmed dish. Dot them with butter and sprinkle Cinnamon Sugar over. Serve the dumplings immediately.

Serves 6–8

VARIATION: Instead of serving the dumplings on their own, serve them with a spicy cinnamon and butter sauce. Add 15 ml butter and a little Cinnamon Sugar (page 21) to the water in which the dumplings were cooked and simmer until the butter has melted. Pour over the hot dumplings and serve.

NOTE: The secret of obtaining light dumplings is to ensure that they are not completely covered by water during steaming.

CHAPTER 8

BISCUITS, SCONES, CAKES AND SWEET TARTS

In the days when everything was made at home, there were usually two baking days a week, when the housewife made all the bread, biscuits and other baked goods for the family's consumption. In the towns, flour – a coarse wholewheat meal – was ground at the local mill, but on farms, the flour was ground by the farm workers. If a small quantity was needed, it was ground in a hand mill. Baking was generally done in an outside oven. The baking pans were put into the oven with a long-handled paddle and when the baked products were ready, they were removed with a curved iron instrument called a rabble. Later on, when the wood-burning iron range became the norm, baking was done inside the house, but the basic baking principles remained essentially the same.

OLD-FASHIONED GINGER BISCUITS

This was one of the staples of grandma's day, when large batches were baked and stored for later use.

100 g golden syrup
75 g lard or margarine
50 g white sugar
5 ml ground ginger
2 ml bicarbonate of soda
250 g self-raising flour

Place all the ingredients, except the flour, in a fairly large saucepan and heat gently until the lard or margarine has melted. Remove the saucepan from the stove and stir in the flour, 30 ml at a time. Roll the mixture into walnut-sized balls and place, 5 cm apart, on greased baking sheets. Bake at 160 °C, above the middle of the oven, for approximately 10 minutes. Leave the biscuits on the baking sheets for a few minutes to firm, then transfer them to a wire rack to cool completely. Store in an airtight container.
Makes about 50

NOTE: The dough may be rolled out and cut with a biscuit cutter if preferred.

TRADITIONAL SPICE BISCUITS

Another standard bake of yesteryear, these biscuits are very similar to the delicious soetkoekies which were decorated with red bolus.

500 g cake flour
15 ml baking powder
5 ml salt
2 ml ground ginger
2 ml ground cinnamon
2 ml ground mixed spice
250 g margarine
250 g white sugar
2 jumbo eggs

Sift the flour, baking powder, salt, ginger, cinnamon and mixed spice into a mixing bowl. Cream the margarine and sugar until light and fluffy. Add the eggs one by one, beating well after each addition. Fold in the flour mixture and mix well. Roll the dough out to 5 mm thick on a lightly floured surface and cut out rounds with a biscuit cutter. Place the rounds on greased baking sheets and bake at 180 °C for approximately 10 minutes.
Makes about 100

HERTZOG COOKIES (HERTZOGGIES)

The story goes that General Hertzog was so fond of these cookies that they were given his name.

30 ml margarine or butter
60 ml white sugar
3 large egg yolks
5 ml vanilla essence
500 g self-raising flour
1 ml salt
a little milk or water

FILLING
250 ml white sugar
3 large egg whites, stiffly beaten
500 ml desiccated coconut
smooth apricot jam

Cream the margarine or butter and sugar until light and creamy. Stir in the egg yolks and vanilla essence, blending well. Sift the flour and salt over the mixture, blend well and then stir in a little milk or water to make a fairly stiff dough. Roll out to about 5 mm thick on a floured surface and cut into rounds with a biscuit cutter. Line greased patty pans with the pastry rounds. To make the filling, gradually add the sugar to the egg whites, beating well to blend. Fold in the coconut. Drop a little apricot jam in the centre of each pastry round and spoon some coconut mixture over it. Bake at 200 °C for approximately 15 minutes, or until the pastry is lightly golden. Cool slightly in the pans, then cool completely on a wire rack. Store the cookies in an airtight container.
Makes about 60

VARIATION: To save time, bake the dough and filling on a baking sheet and cut into squares.

MACAROONS

Macaroons were among the special delicacies the early settlers prepared for the Christmas season, and they are just as popular today.

250 g ground almonds
250 g castor sugar
4 large egg whites
5 ml almond essence
1 ml salt

Mix the almonds and the castor sugar together over low heat. Beat the egg whites until soft peaks form and stir into the almond mixture, off the stove. Fold in the almond essence and the salt. Spoon or pipe a little of the almond mixture at a time onto a baking sheet lined with greased baking paper. Bake at 150 °C for 20–30 minutes. Remove the macaroons from the oven while they are still warm, lift them from the baking paper and cool on absorbent paper. Store in an airtight container.
Makes 12–16

KRAPKOEKIES

Krapkoekies and Hertzog Cookies are long-established in our culinary repertoire.

These traditional Malay biscuits are spicy, with a subtle touch of Dried Naartjie Peel (page 97).

200 g butter
65 ml sunflower oil
250 ml white sugar
1 large egg
500 g cake flour
pinch of salt
7 ml ground cardamom
5 ml ground cinnamon
5 ml ground Dried Naartjie Peel
  (page 97)
250 g desiccated coconut
100 g glacé orange peel,
  cut into squares

Cream the butter, oil and sugar until light and fluffy and the sugar has dissolved. Beat in the egg. Sift the flour, salt, cardamom, cinnamon and naartjie peel and add to the creamed mixture. Mix well. Add the coconut and mix to a fairly stiff dough. Roll out the dough to 6 mm thick on a floured surface and scrape the top with a fork to make a rough texture. Cut into rounds with a biscuit cutter and top each with a piece of glacé orange peel. Place on greased baking sheets and bake at 180 °C for 12–15 minutes, or until golden. Cool the biscuits on wire racks.
Makes about 100

SCONES

Scones with Fresh Apricot Jam (page 128) and Koeksisters

Scones must be one of the most popular bakes ever – probably because they are quick to make and delectable served warm with butter and jam. The cooking methods vary, however, with some being griddle cakes cooked on a flat griddle over the fire rather than baked. Do not overmix the dough or bake scones for too long, or else they will be heavy.

500 ml cake flour
30 ml white sugar
20 ml baking powder
2 ml salt
60 ml butter
200 ml milk or 1 egg mixed
  with 150 ml milk

Sift the flour, sugar, baking powder and salt. Cut in the butter and rub it in lightly with your fingertips until crumbly. Add the milk and mix lightly with a knife – do not knead. Turn the dough out onto a lightly floured board and press into an oblong shape 20 mm thick. Cut into squares or cut out rounds with a biscuit cutter. Place on a greased baking sheet and brush the tops with extra milk or egg and milk. Bake at 240 °C for 10 minutes, or until lightly browned on top. Serve warm with cheese, or jam and cream.
Makes 12

VARIATION: Use 250 ml unsifted wholewheat flour and 250 ml cake flour instead of 500 ml cake flour, and omit the sugar. (Add the wholewheat flour after sifting the dry ingredients.)

Oblietjies
These Dutch rolled wafers, very similar to Brandy Snaps (page 97), were made from a French pastry, with cinnamon and naartjie rind added, and cooked in special long-handled oblietjie irons, which looked much like the old-fashioned waffle irons. They were served with honey and cream.

SCONES MADE WITH OIL

These easy-to-make scones were often referred to as 'drop' scones by our mothers and grandmothers.

500 ml cake flour
20 ml baking powder
2 ml salt
100 ml sunflower oil
1 medium egg
125 ml milk

Sift the flour, baking powder and salt together. Combine the oil, egg and milk and cut into the flour mixture. Do not knead. Mix lightly, then drop tablespoonfuls onto a greased baking sheet. Bake at 240 °C for 10 minutes. Serve warm.

Makes 12

VARIATION: Add 125 ml grated Cheddar cheese after sifting the flour mixture.

CRUMPETS

The British served crumpets for tea, and they are still popular in many parts of our country.

500 ml cake flour
20 ml baking powder
2 ml salt
2 large eggs
60 ml white sugar
250 ml milk
20 ml melted butter

Sift the flour, baking powder and salt into a bowl. Beat the eggs and sugar together, then stir in the milk and butter. Fold in the flour mixture and stir well to form a smooth batter. Fry tablespoonfuls of batter on a hot griddle or in a heavy-based frying pan, turning once. Serve with butter, honey or jam and cream.

Makes 25–30

KOEKSISTERS

Koeksisters are the tamer cousins of Malay sweetmeats, often nut or fruit doughs either boiled or fried in fat and then preserved in honey or a thick syrup of concentrated fruit juices. These sweetmeats were heavily spiced and very sweet – almost too sweet for Western tastes. Many expert koeksister-makers prepare the syrup the night before, so that it has plenty of time to chill.

SYRUP
375 ml water
800 g white sugar
2 ml cream of tartar
1 piece root ginger, bruised
3 sticks cinnamon

DOUGH
500 g cake flour
30 ml baking powder
2 ml salt
60 ml butter or margarine
2 large eggs
250 ml milk
sunflower oil for deep-frying

To make the syrup, heat the water in a saucepan, add the sugar and stir until dissolved (wash down the sugar crystals adhering to the sides of the saucepan). Add the cream of tartar, ginger and cinnamon and boil, uncovered, for 5 minutes. Do not stir. Remove from the stove and chill (see Note). To make the dough, sift the flour, baking powder and salt together into a bowl, then rub in the butter or margarine until the mixture resembles fine crumbs. Beat the eggs and milk together and add to the dry ingredients. Mix the dough well, then knead it lightly for 2 minutes to make it pliable. Cover the basin with waxed paper and leave it for 1 hour. Roll the dough out to 7 mm to 1 cm thick. Cut into strips 8 cm x 40 cm and make 2 vertical cuts in each strip, starting 5 mm from the top and cutting right down to the bottom. Plait the strips loosely and press them together at the loose end. Heat the oil to 190 °C and deep-fry the koeksisters, a few at a time, for 2–4 minutes. Remove from the oil, drain on crumpled brown paper or absorbent paper for about 1 minute, then dip them in the cold syrup for 30 seconds. Remove the koeksisters from the syrup and dry on a wire rack placed on a tray.

Makes about 24

NOTE: As the syrup must remain cold, chill it in two basins and leave one in the refrigerator while the other is being used. Swap them around as soon as the syrup being used starts to get too warm.

WAFFLES

Old-fashioned waffle irons, which consisted of two patterned cast-iron plates on a hinge and with a long handle, were used to cook waffles over the open fire. They can still be seen at numerous museums around South Africa. Electric waffle irons, which seem to be making a comeback, do the job in half the time, but not as decoratively.

500 ml cake flour
10 ml white sugar
20 ml baking powder
2 ml salt
250 ml milk
2 large eggs, separated
50 ml melted butter

Sift the flour, sugar, baking powder and salt together. Gradually add the milk, mixing well. Beat the egg yolks and add them to the batter. Fold in the melted butter. Beat the egg whites until stiff but not dry and fold them into the batter. Pour a thin layer of the batter into the waffle iron, close the iron and cook the waffles for approximately 5 minutes, or until done. Serve the waffles piping hot with honey or golden syrup and cream or ice cream.

Makes about 10

NOTE: Waffles freeze very well. Interleave them with plastic and then overwrap them before freezing. To use the frozen waffles, grill them in the oven for a short while, or pop them into the toaster until they are hot and crisp. Do not thaw them at room temperature or reheat them in the microwave oven – either of these will make them soggy.

SPONGE CAKE

Recipes for sponge cake abound in the old cookery books, many of them using a large number of eggs. Tube pans were used for these light cakes, which had air beaten into the egg whites to make them rise.

120 g cake flour
2 ml salt
5 large eggs, separated
160 g fine granulated sugar
5 ml cream of tartar dissolved in 10 ml water or 15 ml lemon juice

Sift the cake flour and salt together 3 times. Beat the egg whites until stiff but not dry, then gradually beat in 100 g of the sugar and the cream of tartar mixture or lemon juice. Beat the egg yolks in a small bowl until thick and pale yellow. Add the rest of the sugar gradually, beating until the sugar has dissolved. Fold the egg yolks into the egg whites with a spatula or wooden spoon; do not stir. Sift the flour mixture over the eggs in thin layers, folding in lightly after each addition to ensure that the air in the egg mixture is not disturbed. Line the base of an ungreased tube pan or 2 layer cake pans with greased baking paper. Turn the batter into the pan(s) and tap them lightly on the table to break the bigger air bubbles. Bake at 160 °C for 50 minutes to 1 hour, or until the crust is a light golden brown and the cake has shrunk from the sides of the pan and is springy to the touch. Invert the pan(s) onto a cooling rack and leave until almost cold before turning out to cool completely.

Serves 8–10

APRICOT POPOVERS (HANDTERTJIES)

These little mouthfuls of sheer bliss melt in your mouth.

250 g Quick Flaky Pastry (page 100)
smooth apricot jam
castor sugar

Chill the pastry for about 15 minutes, or until firm. Roll out to a large square on a floured surface and cut into 12 squares, 10 cm x 10 cm. Place 5 ml jam on one diagonal half of each square and fold it over into a triangle. Dampen the edges with water and press to seal. Place on greased baking sheets and bake at 180 °C for 30 minutes, or until lightly golden. Remove the tartlets from the oven, sprinkle with castor sugar and leave them to cool slightly.

Makes 12

DRIED NAARTJIE PEEL

No well-stocked 18th or 19th century kitchen was without a jar of dried naartjie peel, which was used to flavour all kinds of dishes. To dry naartjie peels, remove the peel from the fruit in strips and dry in the sun or in the oven at 100 °C until hard. Store in an airtight jar. Use the strips or crush them first, as required in the recipe.

BRANDY SNAPS

Brandy Snaps with whipped cream and Waffles served with golden syrup.

My aunt was famous for two things: her Bobotie (page 45) and her brandy snaps. A variation of brandy snaps called Oblietjies (page 94) was brought to South Africa by the Dutch. The trick to making perfect brandy snaps is to bake only two or three of them at a time, and to work quickly so that they do not set before they have been properly shaped.

65 ml butter or margarine
75 ml castor sugar
60 g black treacle
5 ml lemon juice
125 ml cake flour, sifted
2 ml salt
5 ml ground ginger

Place the butter or margarine, castor sugar, treacle and lemon juice in a saucepan and simmer over moderate heat until the butter has melted, stirring occasionally. Remove from the stove. Add the flour, salt and ginger and mix well. Drop 2–3 teaspoonfuls of the batter, 12 cm apart, on well-greased baking sheets and bake at 190 °C for about 5 minutes, or until a rich brown and well spread out. Remove the baking sheet from the oven and allow the brandy snaps to cool for no more than 1 minute. While still warm, wrap each biscuit around the handle of a wooden spoon to make a roll. Allow them to firm before removing the handle and lifting them onto a wire rack to cool completely. Repeat with the remaining batter. Store in an airtight container until needed, then serve filled with whipped cream laced with brandy.
Makes 18

RICH CHOCOLATE CAKE

20 ml cocoa
30 ml water
125 ml boiling milk
125 ml butter
190 ml castor sugar
5 ml vanilla essence
3 large eggs
120 g cake flour
10 ml baking powder
1 ml salt

DATE AND NUT FILLING
30 ml cocoa powder
125 ml white sugar
125 ml water
15 ml butter
125 ml finely chopped dates
125 ml finely chopped pecan nuts

CHOCOLATE BUTTER ICING
125 g butter or margarine
250 g sifted icing sugar

15–20 ml cocoa or drinking chocolate powder
2 ml vanilla essence

Mix the cocoa to a paste with the water. Add to the boiling milk and stir until smooth. Allow to cool. Beat the butter and castor sugar until light and creamy and the sugar has dissolved completely. Beat in the vanilla essence. Beat the eggs until frothy and fold into the butter mixture. Sift the flour, baking powder and salt together 3 times. Add a little to the butter mixture alternately with a little of the milk mixture and stir until smooth. Continue until all of the flour mixture and milk mixture have been used and the batter is smooth. Beat well and pour into 2 greased and lined 20 cm diameter cake pans. Bake at 190 °C for approximately 30 minutes, or until the cakes recede from the sides of the pans and are springy to the touch. Cool slightly in the pans, then turn them out onto wire racks and cool completely. To make the filling, mix the cocoa, sugar and water in a saucepan, then stir in the butter and dates. Simmer over moderate heat until the mixture is thick and smooth, stirring occasionally. Remove from the stove and cool for 2 minutes, then stir in the nuts. Spread this over 1 layer of the cake. Place the other layer on top. To make the icing, beat the butter or margarine until softened, then work in the icing sugar, cocoa or drinking chocolate and vanilla essence until smooth. Spread over the cake, make a pattern with a fork and leave the cake in a cool place until the icing has set.
Serves 8–10

Swiss Roll and Apricot Popovers are both traditional South Africans treats.

SWISS ROLL (ROLKOEK)

This cake has been enjoyed by countless South Africans for generations.

60 g cake flour
1 ml salt
2 large eggs, separated
100 g white sugar
7 ml lemon juice
smooth apricot jam
sifted icing sugar for sprinkling (optional)

Sift the flour and salt together into a mixing bowl. Beat the egg whites in a large bowl until stiff but not dry. Fold in the egg yolks and beat until thick and pale yellow. Gradually add the sugar and lemon juice, beating constantly. Fold in the flour mixture. Spoon the batter into a swiss roll pan sprayed with non-stick cooking spray. Tilt the pan to spread the batter evenly. Bake at 200 °C for 10 minutes. Spread a damp cloth over a cooling rack and turn the cake out onto it. Spread apricot jam over the cake and roll it up from one short end, using the cloth as a guide. Remove the cloth and leave the cake to cool. Sprinkle the cake with icing sugar if desired.

Serves 6–8

VARIATION: Add 45 ml cocoa powder to the flour and sift with the sugar. Add 50 ml water after folding in the sifted flour mixture. Use whipped cream instead of apricot jam when rolling up the cake.

RICH FRUIT CAKE

Every country has its traditional fruit cake. This is one of the best. Make the cake at least a month in advance, as it needs time to mature before using.

500 g seedless raisins
500 g dates, chopped
250 g sultanas
250 g currants
250 g Candied Peel (page 117)
125 g ginger preserve, chopped
125 g glacé cherries, chopped
75 ml brandy
500 g white sugar
200 ml boiling water
500 g cake flour
2 ml ground mixed spice
2 ml ground cinnamon
2 ml ground ginger
2 ml salt
500 g butter
8 large eggs, beaten
5 ml bicarbonate of soda
15 ml strong coffee
250 g pecan nuts, walnuts or almonds, chopped
brandy, rum or Van der Hum Liqueur (page 142)

Mix the raisins, dates, sultanas, currants, peel, ginger and cherries. Pour the brandy over the mixture and soak overnight. Heat 250 g of the sugar over moderate heat until it starts to brown. Add the boiling water and cool. Sift the flour, spices and salt together. Cream the butter with the remaining sugar. Add a little of the eggs to the creamed mixture alternately with the flour mixture, stirring constantly. Repeat until all the eggs and flour mixture have been added. Add the cooled syrup, then fold in the soaked fruit. Dissolve the bicarbonate of soda in the coffee and add it to the batter with the nuts. Spoon the batter into a large, well-greased cake pan lined with aluminium foil. Cover with foil. Bake for 4–5 hours at 150 °C. Turn out and sprinkle with brandy, rum or Van der Hum liqueur. Store in an airtight container in a cool place, and sprinkle with brandy, rum or liqueur once a week. Leave to mature for at least a month.

Makes 1 large cake

NOTES
- The cake can also be iced, first with marzipan and then with royal icing.
- Fruit cake freezes very well. It can be thawed at room temperature or sliced straight from the freezer – this makes it easier to slice.
- Serve leftover cake with custard as a dessert.

SHORTCUST PASTRY

500 g cake flour
5 ml salt
350 g butter or margarine
175 ml iced water
30 ml lemon juice

Sift the flour and salt into a bowl. Cut or rub the butter or margarine into the mixture until it resembles coarse crumbs. Sprinkle the water and lemon juice over the mixture. Press the dough together lightly – do not knead. Wrap the dough in waxed paper and chill until needed.
Makes 1 kg

NOTE: Bake at 200–230 °C for the length of time specified in the recipe.

VARIATIONS

- Sweet Shortcrust Pastry: Add 40 g sugar to the dry ingredients. Use for sweet tarts.
- Cheese Shortcrust Pastry: Rub 60 g finely grated Cheddar cheese into the flour mixture with the butter.
- Wholewheat Shortcrust Pastry: Use 250 g unsifted wholewheat flour and 250 g cake flour. Add the unsifted flour after the cake flour and salt have been sifted. Use for a savoury tart.
- Cinnamon Shortcrust Pastry: Add 5 ml ground cinnamon to the sifted flour mixture and use this pastry for making apple tart.
- Lemon Shortcrust Pastry: Add 10 ml grated lemon rind to the flour mixture and use for citrus tarts.

QUICK FLAKY PASTRY

500 g cake flour
2 ml salt
7 ml cream of tartar
500 g butter, chilled and grated
150 ml iced water

Sift the flour, salt and cream of tartar together. Rub in the butter lightly with

your fingertips. Cut in the iced water with a knife and place the pastry in the refrigerator for at least 1 hour. Roll the dough out on a floured board. Fold into an envelope shape (see Puff Pastry below) and roll out again. Repeat twice. Use the pastry immediately.
Makes 1 kg

NOTE: If baking flaky pastry blind, bake at 240 °C for 10–15 minutes. If baking with filling, bake at 240 °C for 10 minutes, then reduce the temperature to 190°C.

PUFF PASTRY

250 g cake flour
2 ml salt
15 ml lard
125 ml iced water mixed with 10 ml brandy, or 10 ml lemon juice, or 1 egg yolk
250 g butter, chilled and grated

Sift the flour and salt together twice, then rub in the lard with your fingertips. Cut in the iced water and brandy or lemon juice or egg yolk with a knife. Knead the dough lightly on a floured surface until smooth and elastic and small bubbles form on the surface. Work lightly and quickly to keep the dough cool. Roll the dough out to 5 mm to 1 cm thick on a floured surface. Sprinkle a third of the grated butter over the dough. Fold the dough over from the corners, envelope fashion. Roll out the dough. Repeat, folding twice more. Wrap the dough in waxed paper and chill in the refrigerator before use.
Makes 500 g

NOTES

- Bake at 230–260 °C for 5–10 minutes, then reduce the temperature to 200 °C.
- All the ingredients must be kept as cold as possible to ensure the lightness of the pastry.
- If the dough becomes sticky, refrigerate it for a few minutes to make it pliable.
- Take care not to scorch the pastry, as scorcing will cause it to taste bitter.

MILK TART (MELKTERT)

This has to be the most famous South African sweet tart. Made correctly, it's a sublime taste experience. The recipe can be halved, but it's well worth making two rather than one. Milk tart also reheats very well.

500 g Puff Pastry (page 100) or Quick Flaky Pastry (page 100)

FILLING
7 ml butter
1 ml salt
1 stick cinnamon
750 ml boiling milk
10 ml custard powder
15 ml cornflour
15 ml cake flour
25 ml cold milk
125 ml white sugar
4 large eggs, separated
2 ml almond essence
Cinnamon Sugar (page 21)

Line 2 pie plates with the pastry and make a raised edge for each. To make the filling, add the butter, salt and cinnamon to the boiling milk. Mix the custard powder, cornflour and flour to a paste with the cold milk. Stir in a little of the hot milk mixture. Stir the custard mixture into the hot milk, add 50 ml of the sugar and bring to the boil, stirring continuously. Remove from the stove when it has thickened and discard the cinnamon. Beat the egg whites until stiff but not dry. Gradually beat in the remaining sugar. Beat the egg yolks lightly and stir in a little of the custard mixture. Stir the yolks into the custard mixture, then add the almond essence. Carefully fold in the egg whites. Pour the mixture into the pastry cases and bake at 200 °C for approximately 10 minutes. Lower the temperature to 180 °C and bake for a further 10–15 minutes, or until the filling has set. Cool slightly and sprinkle the tart with cinnamon sugar.

Makes 2 tarts

Milk Tart is the most well-known traditional South African sweet tart.

ALMOND TART

In his diary, Jan van Riebeeck records planting wild almond trees to form a hedge at the settlement. These wild nuts are not edible, but the edible kind were also planted and harvested, and almonds were an important part of many dishes.

125 g Shortcrust Pastry (page 100)

FILLING
50 ml butter or margarine
50 g white sugar
50 g semolina
5 ml almond essence
1 large egg, beaten
2 ml baking powder
30 ml smooth apricot jam

Line an 18 cm diameter pie dish with the pastry. To make the filling, melt the butter or margarine and sugar in a saucepan, stir in the semolina and cook, stirring, for a few minutes. Remove the saucepan from the stove, add the almond essence and stir well to cool the mixture slightly. Add the beaten egg and baking powder and mix well. Spread the jam over the pastry. Pour in the filling and spread it out evenly. Bake the tart at 200 °C for approximately 30 minutes, or until the top is lightly browned.
Serves 6–8

NOTE: If preferred, use some of the pastry to make a latticework pattern on top of the tart. Brush with melted apricot jam to glaze.

VARIATION: Make a number of smaller tartlets instead of one large tart, if you prefer.

LEMON MERINGUE PIE

Instead of this egg, lemon and condensed milk filling, lemon curd is sometimes used for this pie.

1 baked Shortcrust Pastry shell
(page 100)

FILLING
3 large egg yolks
grated rind and juice of 3 lemons
250 g sweetened condensed milk

TOPPING
3 large egg whites
65 ml castor sugar

To make the filling, beat the egg yolks, lemon rind and juice until thick and creamy. Beat in the condensed milk and pour the mixture into the pastry shell. To make the topping, beat the egg whites and castor sugar until stiff but not dry and spoon it over the lemon filling. Bake the pie at 180 °C for 25 minutes. Serve cold.
Serves 6

Clockwise from the top: Almond Tart, Lemon Meringue Pie and Date Loaf with cream.

COCONUT TART (KLAPPERTERT)

Coconut and apricot jam are a favourite combination of ingredients to use in sweet tarts, in both the Malay and the Afrikaner communities.

250 g Shortcrust Pastry (page 100)

FILLING
smooth apricot jam
55 g butter or margarine
65 ml white sugar
1 large egg, beaten with 1 ml salt
250 ml desiccated coconut
1 ml almond essence

Line a 22 cm pie dish with the pastry. To make the filling, spread the jam in the pastry base. Beat the butter or margarine and the sugar until light, making sure that the sugar dissolves completely. Gradually beat in the egg. Stir in the coconut and almond essence and mix well. Spread the mixture over the jam. Bake at 200 °C for 30 minutes.
Makes 1 tart

DATE LOAF

This loaf, served with cream instead of buttered, was my uncle's favourite dessert. He was so fond of it that he begged my grandmother to let him have it before the meal, to make sure he had enough 'space' for it.

250 g dates, chopped
5 ml bicarbonate of soda
250 ml boiling water
15 ml butter or margarine
1 large egg, beaten
100 g cake flour, sifted
80 g walnuts, chopped (optional)
3 ml baking powder
250 g white sugar
3 ml salt

Mix the dates, bicarbonate of soda, boiling water and butter or margarine and allow the mixture to cool slightly. Add the remaining ingredients and mix lightly, then pour the batter into a greased and lined loaf pan. Bake at 180 °C for 1 hour, or until the loaf recedes from the sides of the pan and feels springy to the touch. Cool the loaf in the pan for 5 minutes, then turn it out onto a wire rack to cool completely.
Serves 6–8

BANANA LOAF

125 g butter or margarine
250 ml white sugar
4 ripe bananas, peeled and mashed
2 large eggs
250 g cake flour
2 ml salt
5 ml bicarbonate of soda
65 ml water
7 ml baking powder

Cream the butter or margarine and sugar until light and creamy and the sugar has dissolved. Stir in the bananas and beat to mix thoroughly. Beat in the eggs, one at a time, beating well after each addition. Sift the flour and salt over the mixture and stir it in well. Dissolve the bicarbonate of soda in the water and stir it into the mixture, then stir in the baking powder. Pour the batter into a greased loaf pan and bake at 180 °C for about 45 minutes, or until the loaf recedes from the sides of the pan and is springy to the touch. Cool in the pan for about 5 minutes, then turn the loaf out onto a wire rack to cool completely.
Makes 1 loaf

VARIATION: Add 125 ml chopped pecan nuts or walnuts to the dry ingredients.

CHAPTER 9

BREAD AND RUSKS

Many different kinds of bread are available commercially today, but in the past all bread was home-baked, and on baking day the aroma of the bread in the oven was enough to make your mouth water. Baking your own bread is still a South African tradition, especially in the rural areas. Bread-making, in the days before electric ovens made it easier to control, was a fine art which required great skill and experience. Young girls learnt how to make bread from their mothers: how to knead the dough until it was just right, how to judge the temperature of the wood or coal oven and how to judge when the bread was ready. Making rusks – a way of making bread last longer – is a legacy from the Dutch. Although straight-cut rusks are the classic shape, there are many other kinds and shapes of rusks available today.

PROVING YEAST DOUGHS IN THE MICROWAVE OVEN

The proving time is much reduced if it is done in the microwave oven. Prepare the yeast dough according to the recipe and place it in a large greased bowl. Cover the bowl and microwave at 100 per cent power for 15 seconds to warm the dough. Allow to rest for 10 minutes. Repeat the process 2–3 times, or until the dough has doubled in volume.

POTATO YEAST

Commercial yeasts have greatly simplified bread-making. Our grandmothers and great-grandmothers had to make their own yeast, from fermented grape must, crushed raisins, fermented dough, potatoes, dried hops or, sometimes, an indigenous plant that had similar properties. This recipe is a modern version of the potato yeast they made, improved by making use of active dry yeast.

2 medium potatoes, peeled and grated
500 ml boiling water
30 ml white sugar
10 ml salt
2 ml active dry yeast soaked in 125 ml lukewarm water

Place the potatoes in a glass jar with a screw top. Pour the boiling water into the jar and allow it to cool. Mix the sugar, salt and active dry yeast soaked in lukewarm water and add to the potatoes. Screw the top firmly on the jar, then turn it back one turn to allow some air to get into the jar. Cover and set aside in a warm place for 6–8 hours. Strain off all but 250 ml of the liquid and use as desired. Keep the reserved liquid for 8–10 days, then use as a starter for a new batch of yeast: follow this recipe, omitting the active dry yeast.

MUST BUNS (MOSBOLLETJIES)

Mosbolletjies were a seasonal delicacy in the wine-producing areas, because the yeast relied on grape must. It is not easy to obtain grape must today, but a suitable modern substitute is a yeast made from raisins.

RAISIN YEAST
500 g large raisins (with pips)
1.5 litres water
5 ml active dry yeast (see Note)
30 ml white sugar
500 g bread flour

BUNS
500 g butter or margarine
125 ml boiled milk
4.5 kg cake flour
750 g white sugar
5 ml salt
30 ml aniseed
30 ml sugar dissolved in 250 ml water

To make the yeast, crush the raisins and add to the water in a saucepan. Boil for 15 minutes. Cool until lukewarm. Add the yeast and sugar and stir to dissolve.

Pou into a glass or earthenware bowl and leave, covered, in a warm place for 24 hours, or until the raisins rise to the surface. Strai, then mix in the bread flour until smooth. Leave in a warm place for about 4 hours, or until foamy and well fermented. To make the buns, melt the butter or margarine over low heat and add the boiled milk. Mix into the yeast mixture. Add the cake flour, sugar and salt and enough warm water to make a stiff dough. Stir in the aniseed. Knead the dough for at least 20 minutes, or until bubbles form on the surface. Cover the dough and leave it to rise in a warm place overnight, or until doubled in volume. Shape into buns. Pack them closely together in greased loaf pans. Allow the buns to rise until doubled in volume, then brush them with the sugar and water mixture. Bake at 200 °C for approximately 1 hour. Leave the buns in the pans for about 5 minutes, then turn out and leave them to cool. Serve the buns with butter.
Makes about 60

VARIATION: Break the mosbolletjies into rusks and dry them in the oven at 75 °C for 4 hours. Store them in airtight containers.

NOTE: Active dry yeast needs to be sprinkled onto a lukewarm liquid and left to froth. Instant dry yeast, on the other hand, may be added directly to the dry ingredients. This saves time when preparing the dough, and also shortens the rising time.

BUTTERMILK RUSKS (KARRINGMELKBESKUIT)

1 kg self-raising flour
5 ml baking powder
10 ml salt
2 large eggs
200 ml white sugar
500 ml buttermilk
190 g butter, melted

Sift the flour, baking powder and salt together. Beat the eggs, sugar and buttermilk together. Cut this mixture into the dry ingredients with a knife. Knead the dough lightly, gradually adding the butter while kneading. This will take about 7 minutes. Pack balls of dough tightly into greased loaf pans. (The balls should reach to about two-thirds the height of the pans.) Bake at 180 °C for 30 minutes. Turn out onto a wire rack and break into individual rusks. Lower the oven temperature to 100 °C and dry the rusks for about 4 hours, turning them every 30 minutes. Cool on a wire rack and store in airtight containers. They will keep for at least 3 months.
Makes about 30

Buttermilk Rusks and Must Buns are firm favourites.

TRADITIONAL RUSKS (BOEREBESKUIT)

These traditional rusks use salt-raising yeast dough, also known as soetsuurdeeg.

YEAST
500 ml boiling water
250 ml water
5 ml salt
5 ml white sugar
500–625 ml wholewheat flour

RUSKS
1 litre salt-rising yeast
3 kg bread flour
15 ml salt
125 ml butter melted in 750 ml tepid water

For the yeast, mix all the water, salt and sugar in a deep bucket or saucepan which has a lid. Sprinkle the flour over the liquid and cover the container with the lid. Wrap the container in blankets and leave it in a warm place overnight. To make the rusks, mix the yeast with the flour and salt in a bowl. Add the melted butter and water and knead the dough until it is soft and elastic. Cover the bowl and leave the dough in a warm place to rise for 45 minutes to 1 hour, or until doubled in volume. Shape the dough into small balls and pack them closely together in greased loaf pans. Leave to rise for about 30–45 minutes, or until doubled in volume. Preheat the oven to 190 °C. Bake the buns for approximately 45 minutes or until they are golden. Remove the pans from the oven and allow the buns to cool. Remove the buns and break them into rusks. Dry the rusks in the oven at 100 °C for about 4 hours. Cool completely, then store the rusks in airtight containers for up to 6 months.
Makes about 100

RAISIN BREAD (ROSYNTJIEBROOD)

Hildagonda Duckitt, in her Diary of a Cape Housekeeper, *writes that raisin bread was made for children to eat during a long journey by ox wagon.*

1 kg white bread flour
250 g white sugar
about 5 ml ground cinnamon
about 2 ml freshly grated nutmeg
10 ml ground aniseed (optional)
150 g seedless raisins
60 ml butter or margarine
500 ml Raisin Yeast (see Must Buns, page 106)

Mix the dry ingredients and stir in the raisins. Rub in the butter or margarine and knead the dough with the yeast. Set the dough aside, covered, in a warm place to rise for about 45 minutes, or until doubled in volume. Shape the dough into a loaf and place it in a greased loaf pan. Leave to rise, covered, for 30–45 minutes, or until doubled in volume. Bake at 200 °C for about 1 hour, or until the loaf is golden on top and sounds hollow when tapped. Cool slightly in the pan, then turn the loaf out onto a wire rack to cool completely. Serve sliced, with butter.

Makes 1 loaf

VARIATION: The recipe for mosbolletjies (see Must Buns, page 106) or Pot Bread (page 109) can also be used to make raisin bread. Add the raisins to the basic dough and shape into a loaf for baking.

Clockwise from top left: Pot Bread, Raisin Bread, Salt-rising Yeast Bread and Tomato Soup (page 16)

POT BREAD (POTBROOD)

Pot Bread was once cooked over the fire by travellers into the interior. It was also baked when bread was required in a hurry. Originally bread dough cooked like dumplings with the meat, pot bread has widened in definition to mean any bread that is baked in a pot, and has become a popular braai accompaniment.

10 ml active dry yeast or instant dry yeast (see Note)
10 ml honey
750 ml warm water
1 kg bread flour
10 ml salt
15 ml sunflower oil

Dissolve the yeast and honey in 250 ml of the warm water and add 15 ml of the bread flour. Leave the mixture in a warm place until foamy. Sift the remaining flour and salt together into a bowl. Make a well in the centre and add the yeast mixture. Knead the dough very well, adding the remaining warm water as you knead. This will take 5–10 minutes.

Add the oil and knead it in well. Cover the bowl and leave the dough to rise for 30–45 minutes in a warm place. Knock down the dough (knead again). Grease a flat-bottomed, cast-iron pot, about 25 cm in diameter. Place the dough in the pot and leave it to rise for 30–45 minutes, or until twice the volume. Place the pot in the embers of the braai fire, heaping coals up around it. Bake, covered, for 45 minutes, or until done, heaping coals onto the lid for the last 15 minutes. Turn out the bread, leave it to cool slightly and serve sliced, with butter.
Serves 4–6

VARIATIONS

- To make Askoek (ash bread), bake the bread directly on the coals or in the embers of the braai fire.
- To make Roosterkoek, roll the dough out lightly and cut into cakes. Leave to rise, then braai directly on the grid over the coals.

NOTE: If using instant dried yeast, mix it with the dry ingredients, then add the honey and water, and proceed as described in the recipe.

SALT-RISING YEAST BREAD

YEAST
850 ml boiling water
5 ml white sugar
10 ml salt
480 g unsifted wholewheat flour
250 ml boiling water

BREAD
3 kg bread flour
salt
melted butter

To make the yeast, place the 850 ml boiling water in a small bucket with a tight-fitting lid, or in a glass jar with a lid, then add the sugar and salt. Sprinkle the wholewheat flour over the water. Close the bucket or jar and leave it in a warm place overnight. Stir the 250 ml boiling water into the mixture and leave it for 1 hour, or until foamy. Use immediately. To make the bread, mix the yeast, bread flour and salt to taste. Knead very well, for about 10 minutes, adding hot water if necessary to make a stiff dough. Brush the dough with melted butter. Cover the basin and leave to rise in a warm place for no longer than 45 minutes, or until doubled in volume. Knock down, shape into 2 loaves and place in greased loaf pans. Leave to rise again for about 30–45 minutes. Bake at 200 °C for 45 minutes to 1 hour, or until the loaves are golden and sound hollow when tapped. Turn them out onto a wire rack to cool.
Makes 2 loaves

ROTI

The Indian community introduced the popular roti to this country. Roti is traditionally served with Chicken Breyani (page 38), but the Cape Malays also served it filled with curried mince or vegetables and rolled up.

1 kg bread flour
5 ml baking powder
5 ml salt
about 650 ml water
250 g butter
melted butter or ghee (see Note)

Mix the flour, baking powder and salt together. Add enough water to make a dough that will roll out easily. Roll the dough out thinly on a floured surface. Spread butter on the right-hand two-thirds of the dough.

Fold the left-hand one-third over the central third and then fold the right-hand third over to make three layers. Fold the top edge down to the centre of the dough, and fold up the bottom edge in the same way. Turn the dough over (so that the smooth side is on top) and roll out thinly. Repeat the buttering, folding and rolling until all the butter has been used. Set aside, covered, in a cool place for 2–3 hours. Roll the dough out again and, using a large plate as a guide, cut out rounds. Brush the roti on both sides with melted butter or ghee and fry on both sides in a pan, brushing often with melted butter or ghee to prevent the roti becoming crisp. Stack the roti on a plate and keep warm while making the others.
Makes about 24

NOTE: Ghee is a clarified butter which is used mainly in Indian cookery.

CRACKLING BREAD (KAIINGBROOD)

Crackling – the little bits of solid matter in rendered animal fat – can be made from any animal for slaughter. The farming community made good use of crackling; not only was it employed to make this bread, but it could also be used in rolls and cake.

10 ml active dry yeast
10 ml white sugar
750 ml tepid water
1 kg bread flour
10 ml salt
15 ml soft pork fat
500 g minced crackling (see Note)

Dissolve the yeast and sugar in 250 ml of the water. Cover the bowl and set it aside in a warm place for 1 hour, or until it is foamy. Sift the flour and salt together. Make a well in the centre of the flour mixture and pour in the yeast mixture.

Knead the dough until smooth and elastic and it comes away from your hands, for approximately 10 minutes. Add the remaining tepid water, a little at a time, kneading it in thoroughly. Knead in the pork fat and add the mince crackling. Knead the dough thoroughly. Shape the dough into a loaf and place it in a greased loaf pan. Bake at 180 °C for about 45 minutes to 1 hour, or until the top is lightly browned and the loaf sounds hollow when tapped. Cool slightly in the pan, then turn the loaf out onto a wire rack and cool completely. Serve sliced, with butter.
Makes 1 loaf

NOTE: To make crackling, chop the animal fat and mince it coarsely. Heat the fat in a saucepan with a little water until melted, then fry it until the fat liquefies (renders). The crackling will form by itself. Scoop it from the fat and mince it finely.

VETKOEK

The aroma of freshly-baked bread is almost too much to bear, but as we all know, bread straight from the oven is difficult to cut. The way around the problem is to do what our forefathers did – set aside a ball of dough and fry individual vetkoek in dripping or oil.

250 ml cake flour
5 ml baking powder
2 ml salt
1 large egg
125 ml milk
125 ml sunflower oil

Sift the flour, baking powder and salt together. In a separate bowl, beat the egg lightly. Add the egg to the flour mixture, then add the milk and mix the batter until smooth. Heat the oil in a frying pan and drop spoonfuls of the batter into the oil. Fry the vetkoek for 2–3 minutes on one side, then turn and fry them for 1 minute on the other side. Serve hot, with butter and honey or – for something savoury – with curried mince.
Makes 8–10

VARIATION: Add 150 ml fresh or canned mealie kernels to the egg mixture. Add to the flour mixture and continue as described in the recipe.

From the top: Green Mealie Bread, Vetkoek and Roti served with curried mince.

GREEN MEALIE BREAD

This bread is traditionally packed in metal cocoa cans with lids and steamed on top of the stove, but can also be cooked over the braai coals.

750 ml fresh mealie kernels cut
from the cob
45 ml cake flour
7 ml baking powder
30 ml butter
15 ml white sugar
5 ml salt

Chop the mealie kernels coarsely with a sharp knife or in a food processor and mix them well with the cake flour, baking powder, butter, sugar and salt. Spoon the mixture into two clean cocoa cans (the old-fashioned metal kind with metal lids), seal tightly with the lids and place the cans in a saucepan of boiling water. Steam the bread over moderate heat for approximately 1–1½ hours (2 hours over the coals). Remove the cans from the saucepan, allow them to cool until they are easy to handle and then turn the loaves out of the cans. Serve sliced, with butter.
Makes 2 loaves

CHAPTER 10

SWEETS AND SWEETMEATS

For centuries, all over the world, sweets like toffee, Fudge (page 115) and peanut brittle have been made at home. These sweets, and one or two that are only found here, like Tameletjie (page 115) and Burnt Almonds (page 117), are widely enjoyed by South Africans, and have been for generations. Each country also has its traditional sweetmeats. Originally these were minced meats sweetened with fruits and honey but in time they have become confections made solely from fruit and some sweetening agent. In South Africa, these include sugared fruit leather (vrugtesmeer), Mebos (page 116) and Fruit Rolls (page 117). It was the custom, in many homes, to serve sweetmeats at the end of a meal or with morning coffee, a custom which is coming back into favour with a slight twist – glacé fruits are served with dessert or cheese as the final course of a meal.

TIPS FOR MAKING SWEETS

- Use a medium-sized, heavy-based saucepan, unless the sweets contain a lot of milk or cream (like Fudge, page 115). If they do, use a larger saucepan, as the mixture tends to boil over.
- As sudden heating or cooling will crack the glass of a sugar thermometer, place it in lukewarm water and heat it to boiling point before placing it in the boiling syrup. After use, leave the thermometer in boiling or very hot water until cooled.
- Mix all the ingredients very well before they reach boiling point.
- Make absolutely sure that the sugar dissolves completely before the mixture begins to boil, otherwise the undissolved sugar could form crystals. This is particularly important for crystalline sweets, such as fudge, as even a few crystals can cause the whole mixture to become granular.
- During cooking, it is extremely important to wash down the sides of the saucepan with a small brush dipped in hot water to get rid of the sugar crystals.
- Do not stir the sugar mixtures while they are boiling, unless they have a good deal of milk or cream in them, and even then only stir when absolutely necessary to prevent burning.
- Plunge the base of the saucepan into cold water for a few seconds as soon as the mixture reaches the correct temperature, to prevent the saucepan's heat raising the temperature of the mixture still further.

USING A SUGAR THERMOMETER

It is very much easier to make sweets if you use a sugar thermometer, because you can tell at a glance whether the mixture is ready or not. Before using the thermometer, test it by placing it in a saucepan of hot water. Bring the water to the boil and read the temperature on the thermometer. Water boils at 100 °C at sea level, but at a few degrees lower at higher altitudes. This difference should be taken into account. If the reading on your thermometer is 3 °C less than the boiling point at sea level, for example, subtract 3 °C from the required temperature for the recipe. For the best results, use the Cold Water Test (below) in conjuction with the sugar thermometer.

COLD WATER TEST

When the syrup reaches the soft-ball stage, it forms a very soft ball when a little of it is dropped into cold water, and the ball flattens when it is removed from the water. At the firm-ball stage, the syrup forms a firm ball when dropped into cold water, and it does not flatten when removed. The temperature of the syrup at sea level varies according to which stage the syrup has reached. At the soft-ball stage it is 112–116 °C, and at the firm-ball stage 118–120 °C.

COCONUT ICE

A traditional Malay sweet, called lallimala, is similar to coconut ice, but much softer in consistency.

150 ml each water and milk, or
300 ml milk
1 kg white sugar
30 ml butter
250 g desiccated coconut
5 ml vanilla essence
few drops of red food colouring
or cochineal

Pour the water and milk (or milk only) into a medium-sized saucepan and add the sugar and butter.

Heat over low heat until the sugar dissolves completely. Bring to the boil and cook for 10 minutes, or until the mixture reaches the firm-ball stage (see Cold Water Test, page 114), stirring occasionally. Meanwhile, oil a shallow, 20 cm-square pan. Remove the saucepan from the stove and add the coconut and vanilla essence. Beat the mixture briskly with a wooden spoon until it is fairly thick and creamy. Pour half into the oiled pan. Add the colouring to the remaining half (do this quickly, as the mixture thickens rapidly, making it difficult for the colour to spread evenly). Pour the pink coconut mixture on top of the white and spread it evenly. Leave the coconut ice in a cool place until firm, then cut it into narrow bars about 4 cm long. Store in an airtight container.
Makes about 1 kg

FUDGE

Popular sweet treats: Fudge, Coconut Ice and Nutty Toffee.

As children, my sister and I were always experimenting with sweet recipes – and always burning ourselves with the hot mixtures. Then we tried this recipe, which has been in the family for generations, and for the first time we were able to savour the (sweet) results of our labours without having to resort to the first aid box.

1 kg white sugar
250 g butter
410 g can evaporated milk
100 ml cold water
1 ml vanilla essence

Rinse a 4 litre saucepan with cold water. Place all the ingredients in the saucepan and heat over low heat until the sugar has dissolved completely, stirring occasionally and brushing down the sides of the pan when necessary. When the sugar has dissolved, bring the mixture to the boil and boil rapidly until it reaches the soft-ball stage (see Cold Water Test, page 114). Remove from the stove and cool for 3 minutes, then beat rapidly with a wooden spoon until it thickens and feels rough. Line a 20 cm-square pan with waxed paper. Pour in the fudge and, when it starts to set, mark it into squares with a knife. Cool completely, cut into squares and store in an airtight container.
Makes about 1 kg

NUTTY TOFFEE (TAMELETJIE)

A very sticky toffee, often called stick-jaw, which has been enjoyed at the Cape since the time of the French Huguenots. Years ago, these sweets were sold by Malay street vendors, but these days they seem to be made only for special private feasts. Pine kernels are the nuts used traditionally (the sweet is then called pitjietameletjie), but as these are exorbitantly expensive today, almonds or desiccated coconut can be used instead.

400 g white sugar
250 ml water
pine kernels, almonds or
desiccated coconut

Boil the sugar and water until the mixture is a caramel colour and starts frothing. Add a sprinkling of chopped pine kernels, almonds or desiccated coconut. Pour into a well-greased, 23 cm-square flat pan and mark off squares with a wet knife. Leave to cool, then cut. Store in an airtight container.
Makes about 400 g

GLACÉ FRUITS

The Dutch colonists were extremely hospitable. Visitors to the homestead were offered coffee and glacé fruits as a sustaining snack.

500 g fruit (see Notes)
30 ml slaked lime dissolved in
5 litres water
1 litre boiling water
500 g white sugar
1 ml cream of tartar

Wash the fruit, prick it with a skewer and chop, segment or leave it whole, depending on the fruit (see Notes). Soak overnight in the lime solution (see Notes), then drain the fruit and rinse it well under cold running water. Cook the fruit in the boiling water for 20–30 minutes (depending on the fruit), or until just tender. Strain the cooking liquid and add 750 ml to the sugar in a saucepan. Stir in the cream of tartar. Bring to the boil to make a syrup. Gradually add the fruit to the boiling syrup. Boil for 30 minutes, then remove from the stove and set aside, covered, overnight. The next day, remove the fruit with a slotted spoon and bring the syrup to the boil. Replace the fruit and boil it again for 30 minutes. Repeat this process for 5–6 days, or until the fruit is saturated with syrup. Drain the fruit and leave it on a wire rack for a few days to dry, turning often to ensure even drying.
Makes about 500 g

NOTES
- Figs, pineapple, smooth-skinned peaches, pears, apricots and citrus fruits are best for making glacé fruit. Leave small figs whole, slice pineapple, pears and citrus fruits (remove the pips) and halve and stone apricots and peaches.
- Soaking in a lime solution makes fruit crisp.

MEBOS

This traditional Cape delicacy combines sweet and sour flavours admirably, but is definitely an acquired taste!

unblemished, ripe apricots
1 kg salt dissolved in 8 litres water
750 g sugar per 500 g mebos

Soak the apricots overnight in the salted water. Next day, drain the apricots and remove the skins. Leave the whole apricots in the sun for 12 hours, then gently force the stones out at one end. If the apricots are small, press 2–3 together into a round, flat shape. Dry them, spread out on racks, for a few days. During the drying process, shape the mebos by hand (dip your hands in a mixture of 30 ml salt and 2 litres water). Weigh the mebos to determine how much sugar you will need. Pack alternate layers of the mebos and sugar neatly into small boxes. Close the boxes securely and store the mebos in a dark place. It will keep for several months.

Traditional ways with fruit: Fruit Rolls, Mebos and Glacé Fruits.

CANDIED PEEL

Our grandmothers used candied peel as a sweet snack or to decorate cakes or desserts.

1 orange
1 lemon
1 grapefruit
250 g white sugar
500 ml water

Wash the fruit and cut into sections. Scoop out the flesh and cut the peel into strips. Soak the orange and lemon peel overnight in water to cover; the grapefruit peel should be soaked for 3 days, changing the water daily. Drain the citrus peel, then boil it in fresh water to cover for 30 minutes, or until soft. (Test with a skewer.)

Boil the sugar and water together until slightly thickened to make a syrup. (It should cover the peel – double the quantities if more is needed.) Bring to the boil and add the peel. Boil again briefly, then cool the peel in the syrup. Repeat the boiling and cooling process 3–4 times, then remove the peel with a slotted spoon and leave to dry on waxed paper.
Makes about 250 g

VARIATIONS

- For a shiny product, glaze the peel. Prepare a syrup using 400 g sugar, 250 ml water and 1 ml cream of tartar. Boil the syrup to the soft-ball stage (see Cold Water Test, page 114). Dip the candied peel in the syrup and place it on waxed paper to dry. Keep the syrup hot while dipping the peel.
- Melt 50 g chocolate with 5 ml butter and dip the candied peel in the chocolate mixture. Place the peel on waxed paper and leave it to dry.

BURNT ALMONDS

Almonds were eaten fresh or sugared and were very often prepared this way. Before cochineal was available, red bolus was used as a colouring for food.

1 kg yellow sugar
10 ml red bolus (see Note) or a few drops of cochineal
15 ml butter
375 ml water
15 ml cake flour
30 ml milk
2 ml salt
10 ml ground ginger
750 ml shelled almonds

Combine the sugar, red bolus or cochineal, butter and water in a heavy-based saucepan and stir over low heat until the sugar has dissolved. Boil to the soft-ball stage (see Cold Water Test, page 114). Mix the flour with the milk and add to the boiled mixture with the salt and ginger. Remove from the stove and beat with a wooden spoon until cool. Add the nuts immediately and drop spoonfuls of the mixture onto a greased baking sheet. Leave to harden. Store in an airtight container.
Makes about 750 g

NOTE: Red bolus is obtainable from pharmacies.

FRUIT ROLLS

Another traditional sweetmeat that's very easy to make.

fresh apricots or peaches, stoned
250 ml sugar per 250 ml minced fruit
butter

Mince the fresh apricots or peaches, or process them very finely in a food processor. Measure the frut to determine how much sugar you will need.

Add the sugar to the minced fruit and mix. Grease waxed paper or baking parchment with butter and spread the fruit mixture evenly over the paper. Leave the fruit to dry in the sun for about 12 hours. Loosen the fruit from the paper and discard the paper. Sprinkle the fruit with sugar and roll up tightly. Store, wrapped in waxed paper, in a cool, dark place. Fruit rolls will keep for several months.

VARIATIONS: Fruit rolls may also be made with guavas, quinces, nectarines, figs, apples or pears.

CHAPTER 11

PRESERVES, JAMS AND JELLIES

Sugar, an ingredient we couldn't do without nowadays to produce preserves, jams and jellies, was not produced locally at the Cape, and had to be imported – at great expense. The colonists were nothing if not inventive, however, and they overcame the lack of sugar by using honey and the concentrated juice of sweet fruits like grapes, cherries and plums instead. In the days before refrigeration and canned goods, preserving fruit and vegetables – as well as making jams, jellies, pickles and chutneys – was a good way to store the bounty of summer for the long winters and also provided a way of using up a glut.

WARMING THE SUGAR

If the sugar is warmed first, the end product turns out very much clearer, because the faster the sugar dissolves, and the faster the preserve, jam, or jelly reaches setting point, the better it will look.

- Spread the sugar in a baking dish. The sugar should be about 3 cm deep.
- Place the baking dish in a slow oven (100 °C) for approximately 10 minutes, stirring occasionally to spread the warmth evenly.
- Alternatively, you can warm the sugar in the microwave oven. Microwave at 100 per cent power for about 30 seconds.

STERILIZING JARS FOR PRESERVES

There are a number of ways to sterilize jars which are to be used for preserves:

- Fill clean jars with warm water and screw on the lids. Place jars on an asbestos mat in the oven at 100–120 °C for 20 minutes. Remove from the oven and pour out the water, then add the fruit.
- Fill clean jars with lukewarm water, leaving 10 mm headspace. Screw on the lids. Place on a trivet or false bottom in a large, deep saucepan and fill the saucepan with warm water. Bring the water to the boil and boil for 10 minutes. Remove the jars with tongs and pour out the water. Fill with fruit.
- Pour a little water into 2–3 jars and microwave at 100 per cent power for up to 5 minutes, depending on the size of the jars. Pour the water out and invert the jars to drain. Do not microwave more than 3 jars at a time, and never sterilize metal lids in the microwave oven; dip them in boiling water.

STERILIZING JARS FOR JAMS AND JELLIES

Place empty jars and their glass lids on an asbestos mat in the oven at 100–120 °C and leave for about 15–20 minutes. Remove the jars from the oven when ready to fill. Sterilize metal lids in boiling water.

STRAINING THE JUICE

To strain the juice for jelly-making, use a sterilized jelly bag or line a sieve with a layer of muslin, then a layer of cotton wool and another layer of muslin. Suspend the bag or sieve over a large bowl and pour in the juice and pulp, a little at a time. Allow the juice to drip through at its own pace. Never squeeze the pulp in the bag to hasten proceedings; the result will be a cloudy jelly.

TESTING JELLIES FOR PECTIN

- Pour 10 ml strained juice into a cup and allow it to cool. Add 10 ml methylated spirits and leave for a few seconds – do not stir. If a large clot forms, the fruit is rich in pectin; if there are two or three lumps, the juice contains a moderate amount of pectin; but if a lot of little clots form, the fruit is low in pectin. To rectify the situation, lemon juice may be added to the fruit juice, or else commercial pectin or Home-made Apple Pectin (page 125).
- If the juice has a high pectin content, add 200 g white sugar for every 250 ml juice, but if it has a moderate pectin content, add 150 g white sugar for every 250 ml juice.

TESTING IF JAMS AND JELLIES ARE READY

There are two methods. Either use a sugar thermometer – the temperature of the jam or jelly should be 105 °C – or remove the jam or jelly from the stove, spoon a little onto a chilled saucer and allow it to cool. If it is ready, the surface should crinkle when it is pushed with a finger.

SEALING JARS WITH PARAFFIN OR CANDLE WAX

- The solidified wax prevents air reaching the jam or jelly and causing decay.
- Fill the jars to within 4 mm of the top and allow the jam, preserve or jelly to set.
- Cut the wax into small pieces and melt it in a double boiler over hot water.
- Pour a layer of melted wax over the contents of the jars to cover the surface completely. Allow the wax to harden, then seal the jars.
- Paper discs dipped in brandy may also be used, but make sure that they cover the surface completely.

Preserving is a good way of using excess fruit, and preserves are enjoyed with bread or scones.

CITRON PRESERVE

Preserves − whole or large pieces of fruit cooked in a sugar syrup − are known colloquially in South Africa as 'konfyt' (the name is thought to be a corruption of the French confiture) and are enjoyed with bread, scones and, more recently, as an accompaniment to cheese or ice cream as a dessert course. Citrons, large, yellowish-green citrus fruits, were among the most popular fruits used by our grandmothers and great-grandmothers for making preserves.

1 kg citrons
1.75 litres boiling water
1 kg white sugar

Scrape the citrons with a grater to remove the shiny green outer skin containing the bitter oil glands, or remove the rind very thinly with a sharp knife. Halve the citrons and remove the flesh, using a sharp-edged teaspoon. Discard the flesh or keep it to make a pungent jelly. Quarter the skins and leave them overnight in a deep basin with enough water to cover. (The skins are light and will float to the top, so weigh them down with a heavy plate and a weight.) Next day, discard the water and weigh the fruit skins − you should have about 750 g. If not, adjust the quantity of sugar in proportion. Immerse the fruit in the boiling water in a large, heavy-based saucepan piece by piece so that the temperature of the water is not reduced. Boil until a skewer or sharpened matchstick will pierce the skins easily, then lift them out with a slotted spoon. Strain the cooking liquid through a jelly bag or muslin-lined sieve (see Straining the Juice, page 120), measure 1.25 litres into a preserving pan (top up with fresh water if there is too little) and bring to the boil. Gradually add the sugar, then reduce the heat and cook, stirring frequently, until a thin syrup forms. Boiling the syrup rapidly, add the fruit slowly so that the temperature is not reduced. (If the syrup has any impurities it should be strained through muslin and brought to the boil again befoe the fruit is added.) Reduce the temperature and cook the fruit slowly so that the syrup does not thicken too soon, otherwise the fruit will be hard and tough. When the syrup boils in small bubbles (about 45 minutes to 1 hour), test a little on a saucer. If, after rapid cooling, it is as thick as cooling dessert jelly, the pan is ready to be removed from the stove. Stir the preserve very gently for approximately 1−2 minutes so that there is no foam on top, then pack the fruit in hot, dry, sterilized jars. Fill the jars with the syrup and allow to cool. When cooled, insert a knife down the inside of each jar to release any air bubbles. Cover the preserve with a paper disc dipped in brandy (see Sealing Jars with Paraffin or Candle Wax, page 120) and seal. Store the preserve in a cool, dark place.

Makes about 1 kg

WATERMELON PRESERVE (WAATLEMOENKONFYT)

This traditional South African favourite is made with preserving watermelon, generally available from fresh produce markets. If you cannot find it, use ordinary watermelon instead.

1 preserving or ordinary watermelon
30 ml slaked lime or 60 ml bicarbonate
of soda per 5 litres water
boiling water to cover

SYRUP
1 kg white sugar per 1 kg skins
2 litres water per 1 kg white sugar
20 ml lemon juice per 1 kg skins
pinch of salt
2 pieces root ginger, bruised,
per 1 kg skins

Slice the watermelon, discarding the soft flesh. Peel the hard green rind off thinly and discard it. Cut the remaining skins into squares, prick well on both sides, then weigh and calculate how much sugar to use for the syrup. Soak the skins in slaked lime or bicarbonate of soda solution for 2 days (12–18 hours for ordinary watermelon). Rinse well and soak in fresh water for 2 hours. Drain and place in boiling water to cover in a large, heavy-based saucepan, one at a time. Boil, uncovered, until just tender; they should be easy to pierce with a matchstick. To make the syrup, combine the sugar, water, lemon juice, salt and ginger in a saucepan over low heat and bring to the boil as soon as the sugar has dissolved. Place the skins in the boiling syrup and boil rapidly until they are tender and translucent and the syrup is thick. Pack into hot, dry, sterilized jars, fill with syrup and seal immediately. The fruit should be firm and shiny but not too dark.

NOTE: The skins can also be boiled in syrup over 3 days. Boil for 30 minutes on the first day and leave to cool. Next day, remove the fruit and bring the syrup to the boil. Add the pieces one by one and boil for 30–40 minutes. Repeat the process the next day, but then boil until ready for packing into jars.

Green Fig Preserve (top), Watermelon Preserve (bottom left) and Orange Preserve (right).

GREEN FIG PRESERVE (GROENVYEKONFYT)

Fig trees grow extremely well in most parts of South Africa, and the crop is prolific. This preserve was traditionally made from the 'first' green figs on the tree. The 'second' crop of figs was reserved for eating fresh and for making Ripe Fig Jam (page 128).

plump green figs
30 ml slaked lime per 5 litres water

SYRUP
1.5 litres water per 1 kg white sugar
1.25 white sugar per 1 kg fruit
20 ml lemon juice per 1 kg fruit
1 piece root ginger, bruised (optional)

Weigh the figs and calculate how much sugar will be needed for the syrup. Scrape the figs with a knife and make a cross on the blossom end of each. Make the slaked lime solution and soak the figs in it overnight. Rinse the figs thoroughly in fresh water and leave them to soak in fresh water for about 15 minutes. To make the syrup, boil the water and pour it over the sugar in a large, heavy-based saucepan. Add the lemon juice and the piece of bruised root ginger, if using, and bring the mixture to the boil, stirring to dissolve the sugar. Meanwhile, boil the figs in water to cover for approximately 15 minutes, or until they are just tender. They are ready if a matchstick can pierce the skin easily. Remove the figs with a slotted spoon and add them to the boiling syrup. Boil, uncovered, until the figs are tender and translucent and the syrup is thick (test the figs with a matchstick). Spoon the figs and the syrup into hot, dry, sterilized jars and seal immediately.

ORANGE PRESERVE

My grandmother used to get oranges from Citrusdal, which she made into this marvellously tangy preserve. It was served with freshly baked Salt-rising Yeast Bread (page 109) and fresh farm butter.

1 kg ripe, firm oranges
salt
boiling water

SYRUP
1.5 kg white sugar
2 litres water
20 ml lemon juice

Thinly grate the rind from the oranges and rub the fruit with salt. Leave the oranges to stand for approximately 30 minutes. Place the oranges in a basin and pour boiling water over them. Leave them until the water has cooled, then drain the oranges and rinse in cold water. Leave to soak overnight in fresh cold water. Cut a deep, narrow cross in the base of each orange. Roll the orange gently between your hands to squeeze out the pips. Place the oranges in enough boiling water to cover in a large, heavy-based saucepan and boil them until the skin is soft; it should be easy to pierce them with a matchstick. (The skin must be soft before boiling the oranges in the syrup, otherwise the preserve will be tough.) Leave the oranges whole, otherwise halve or quarter them as desired. To make the syrup, dissolve the sugar in the water in a large, heavy-based saucepan over low heat. Add the lemon juice and bring to the boil. Add the fruit and boil until the oranges are translucent and the syrup is thick. Skim the foam from the surface, if necessary. Pack the oranges into hot, dry, sterilized jars. Fill the jars with the syrup, covering the fruit completely, and seal immediately.
Makes about 2 kg

APRICOTS IN BRANDY (BOEREMEISIES)

In the early days of the Dutch settlement at the Cape, fruit preserved in brandy – like boeremeisies and Kaapsche jongens – was served on special occasions.

500 g dried or fresh apricots
140 g white sugar
brandy to cover

Mix the apricots and sugar together and add sufficient brandy to cover. Pack into hot, dry, sterilized jars and leave to mature for at least 14 days before use.
Makes about 500 g

PRICKLY PEAR PRESERVE

The fruit of the prickly pear is delicately flavoured and makes a good preserve.

1 kg ripe, firm prickly pear fruits
30 ml slaked lime per 5 litres water

SYRUP
750 g white sugar
1 litre water
30 ml lemon juice

Peel the fruit with a knife and fork and leave whole (take care not to prick yourself with the thorns). Prick the fruit and soak overnight in the lime solution. Rinse thoroughly in fresh water. To make the syrup, dissolve the sugar in the water in a large, heavy-based saucepan over low heat. Add the lemon juice and bring to the boil. Place the fruit in the boiling syrup, a few at a time, and boil, uncovered, until the fruit is translucent and the syrup is thick. Pack the fruit into hot, dry, sterilized jars, fill the jars with the syrup and seal them immediately.
Makes about 1 kg

VARIATION: Use fresh gherkins instead of prickly pears to make Gherkin Preserve (agurkiekonfyt).

FIGS IN PORT

Our ancestors were fond of preserving fruits in brandy, but this modern adaptation combines figs very successfully with port.

200 g white sugar
325 ml water
10 whole cloves
pared and thinly sliced rind of 1 lemon
500 ml port
1 kg fresh, ripe figs

Place the sugar, water and cloves in a large, heavy-based saucepan. Bring to the boil, stirring until the sugar has dissolved, then reduce the heat and simmer for approximately 5 minutes. Add the lemon rind and the port. Pack the figs in hot, dry, sterilized jars and pour the syrup over them, including the lemon rind and cloves. Cover and seal.
Makes about 1.5 kg

VARIATION: Use sherry instead of port.

QUINCE PASTE

Quinces are an old-fashioned fruit, used extensively by our grandmothers to make all kind of preserves. This fruit leather (vrugtesmeer) kept for ages and was served with coffee at the end of a meal.

2 kg quinces
300 ml water
white sugar
castor sugar

Wash the quinces, cut them into quarters and place them in a large, heavy-based saucepan with the water. Simmer for approximately 1 hour, or until the quinces are soft, then press the pulp through a sieve. Weigh the pulp and place it in a large clean saucepan. Weigh an equal quantity of white sugar and mix it into the fruit pulp. Stir the mixture continuously over low heat until the sugar dissolves. Continue cooking until the mixture becomes very thick, stirring constantly. Pour the paste into shallow pans lined with waxed paper and leave the pans in a warm place for about 3–4 days to dry out (this will make it easier to handle the paste). Peel off the paper and cut the paste into pieces. Roll each piece of paste in castor sugar and store the pieces between layers of waxed paper in an airtight container.
Makes about 500 g

KUMQUAT PRESERVE

Kumquats are small, oval citrus fruits which make marvellous preserves and marmalades.

1 kg ripe, firm kumquats
30 ml bicarbonate of soda per 1 litre
boiling water

SYRUP
1 kg white sugar
2 litres water
20 ml lemon juice

Thinly scrape off the rind and place the fruit in a saucepan. Cover with boiling water and bicarbonate of soda solution. Leave to cool, then drain. Cut a cross in the base of each fruit and roll it carefully to remove the pips (take care not to squash the kumquats). Place the fruit in boiling water to cover and boil until just tender but not mushy. To make the syrup, bring the sugar, water and lemon juice to the boil in a large, heavy-based saucepan. Add the fruit and boil until the kumquats are translucent and the syrup thick. Pack the fruit into hot, dry, sterilized jars, fill with the syrup and seal.
Makes about 1.75 kg

MICROWAVE OVEN: Combine the water and sugar for the syrup in a large bowl and microwave at 100 per cent power for 10 minutes. Stir every 2–3 minutes. Strain the syrup through muslin or a sieve to ensure that it is clear. Microwave at 100 per cent power for 3–4 minutes. Add the prepared kumquats and lemon juice. Microwave at 100 per cent for about 15 minutes. Spoon the kumquats and syrup into hot, dry, sterilized jars, leave to cool and seal tightly.

Kumquat Preserve and ice cream with Apricots in Brandy (page 123).

HOME-MADE APPLE PECTIN

1 kg healthy cooking apples,
not quite ripe
1 litre water

Wash and chop the whole apples. Boil them in the water, covered, until just soft. Strain the juice (see Straining the Juice, page 120). Boil the juice again, uncovered, until reduced to 500 ml. Use immediately to increase the pectin value of other juice when making jellies or jams, or bottle and seal for later use. Home-made pectin will keep for 3–4 months.
Makes 500 ml

OLD-FASHIONED MINCEMEAT

Fruit mincemeat was originally made from meat (beef or tongue) mixed with dried fruit, lots of spices and brandy or some other spirit. Beef suet has replaced the meat, and fruit mincemeat nearly always contains apples nowadays. For the best results, allow fruit mincemeat to mature for at least 2 weeks before use. This recipe makes unstinting use of rich and costly ingredients, but it can easily be halved or quartered.

750 g beef suet
500 g seedless raisins
500 g sultanas
675 g apples, cored and chopped
675 g pears, cored and chopped
350 g almonds, blanched and chopped
juice and grated rind of 2 oranges
juice and grated rind of 2 lemons
15 ml mixed spice
675 g soft brown sugar
300 ml brandy
300 ml sherry
300 ml port
300 ml rum

Mix all the ingredients together and pack into hot, dry, sterilized jars. Seal and store for up to 2 months in the refrigerator.
Makes 5.5 kg

From left: Old-fashioned Mincemeat, Tomato Jam and Grape Must Jam.

TOMATO JAM

1 kg jam tomatoes or cherry tomatoes
750 g white sugar
20–25 ml lemon juice

Pour boiling water over the tomatoes, leave for 1 minute and then drop the tomatoes in cold water. Pull off the skins and chop the tomatoes.

Layer the tomatoes and sugar in a large, heavy-based saucepan, add the lemon juice and set the mixture aside, covered, for 2 hours or overnight. Heat the mixture over low heat until the sugar has dissolved, then bring it to the boil and boil over moderate heat until setting point is reached (see Testing if Jams and Jellies are Ready, page 120). Stir from time to time to prevent burning. Skim the surface, if necessary, and pour the jam into hot, dry, sterilized jars. Seal immediately.
Makes about 1 kg

BRANDIED PLUMS

1.5 kg plums
150 g white sugar
8 whole cloves
1 stick cinnamon
1 piece root ginger, crushed
750 ml brandy

Pack the plums into hot, dry, sterilized jars. Add the sugar, cloves, cinnamon and ginger to the brandy in a saucepan and stir until the sugar has dissolved. Bring to the boil. Remove the cinnamon, ginger and cloves and pour the mixture over the plums. Seal the jars immediately. Use after 3 months.
Makes about 1.5 kg

CITRUS MINCEMEAT

This modern version of fruit mincemeat is less costly and more tart than the old-fashioned mincemeat.

thinly grated rind and juice of
2 large lemons
4 cooking apples, peeled, cored and
finely diced
500 g currants
50 g Candied Peel (page 117), chopped
250 g white sugar
2 ml freshly grated nutmeg
1 ml ground mace
pinch of salt

250 g beef suet, finely shredded
50 ml brandy or Van der Hum Liqueur (page 142)

Place the lemon rind and juice, fruits, candied peel, sugar, spices and salt in a saucepan and simmer for 5 minutes. Add the suet and brandy or liqueur, mix thoroughly and pack into hot, dry, sterilized jars. Cover tightly and leave to mature for at least 2 weeks before use. It will keep, securely covered, for up to 6 months in the refrigerator.
Makes about 2 kg

GRAPE MUST JAM (MOSKONFYT)

A delicacy from the wine-making areas of the Cape, this jam was usually served on slices of home-baked bread spread with dripping or lard.

ripe sweet grapes
10 ml slaked lime per 5 litres grape juice

Remove the grapes from their stalks, place in a large bowl, then crush them. Cover the bowl and leave until the grapes ferment, which will take a couple of days. When the skins have risen to the surface,

strain the juice through a sieve and add the slaked lime. Allow the mixture to stand for about 30 minutes. Skim the juice and strain it (see Straining the Juice, page 120). Heat the strained juice to boiling point in a large, heavy-based saucepan and strain it again. Return to the saucepan and boil rapidly, skimming the surface if necessary. Test the jam for setting point (see Testing if Jams and Jellies are Ready, page 120). It should have the consistency of thick syrup. Pour the jam into hot, dry, sterilized jars and seal immediately.

GRAPES IN BRANDY (KAAPSCHE JONGENS OR KORRELBRANDEWYN)

Raisins preserved in brandy were called boerejongens.

ripe, firm Hanepoot grapes
375 ml brandy

SYRUP
200 g white sugar
250 ml water

Wash the grapes carefully and remove the berries from the stalks, leaving a small stalk attached to each grape. Prick with a sterilized needle. To make the syrup, boil the sugar and water together until it has thickened. Remove from the stove and add the brandy. Pack the grapes firmly into hot, dry, sterilized jars and top up with syrup. Seal the jars loosely and sterilize in a waterbath (see Grape Juice, page 140). Remove from the stove and seal tightly. Leave to mature for at least 3 months before use.

MELON AND GINGER JAM

Melon and ginger jam always reminds me of my school days because, almost invariably, this is what was on my sandwiches. I loved it. That was the store-bought variety; there's absolutely no comparison to this well-flavoured home-made jam, which I love even more.

1 kg white sugar
1 kg watermelon, peeled, seeded and diced
50 g preserved ginger, diced
juice of 3 lemons

Sprinkle the sugar over the diced watermelon and ginger.

Cover the dish and leave the mixture to stand overnight. Place in a large, heavy-based saucepan and heat slowly, stirring occasionally, to dissolve the sugar. Add the lemon juice and boil until the jam has set, for about 30 minutes. Test (see Testing if Jams and Jellies are Ready, page 120). Leave to cool for approximately 10 minutes, then pack the jam into hot, dry, sterilized jars and seal.
Makes about 1 kg

FRESH APRICOT JAM

In old manuscripts you will often find remedies for appelkoossiekte (apricot sickness, or an upset stomach) which, they said, was caused by eating too many ripe apricots. It is certainly true that fresh apricots are delicious, but if you are afraid that you will fall prey to this illness, why not make the jam instead?

1 kg firm, ripe apricots, halved and stoned
75 ml water
750 g white sugar
15 ml Van der Hum Liqueur (page 142)

Place the apricots and the water in a large, heavy-based saucepan and simmer, covered, for approximately 10 minutes,

or until the fruit is tender. Add the sugar and heat slowly, stirring occasionally, until the sugar has completely dissolved. Boil the mixture rapidly until setting point is reached (see Testing if Jams and Jellies are Ready, page 120) and skim, if necessary, to remove foam from the surface. Cool the jam slightly, then stir in the Van der Hum liqueur. Pour the jam into hot, dry, sterilized jars, cover with melted wax (see Sealing Jars with Paraffin or Candle Wax, page 120) and seal the jars immediately.
Makes about 1.5 kg

RIPE FIG JAM

Ripe fig jam always reminds me of my grandparents' home in Worcester. There were a number of gnarled old fig trees in the garden that bore masses of fruit, which meant that my grandmother always had rows of the jam on the pantry shelf.

1.5 kg ripe figs, peeled
250 ml water
750 g white sugar
60 ml lemon juice

Weigh the figs. Boil them in the water in a large, heavy-based saucepan until tender.

Mash or purée the figs, then add the sugar and lemon juice, and proceed as for Fresh Apricot Jam (above).
Makes about 1.5 kg

MICROWAVE OVEN: Wash the unpeeled figs well, then slice them. Place the figs in a large plastic container with the other ingredients and leave, covered, overnight. Microwave at 100 per cent power for 1 hour. Pour the jam into hot, dry, sterilized jars and seal.

SOUR FIG JAM (SUURVYEKONFYT)

The sour fig is a wild succulent with fruit which tastes sour if eaten raw. Sour figs grow on the sandy dunes all around our coastline, but are mostly found in the Cape and along the south coast of KwaZulu-Natal. The fruit of the sour fig is available throughout the year. Although they are most unprepossessing-looking little fruits, they make an unexpectedly delicious jam.

1 kg fresh sour figs
100 g salt dissolved in 5 litres water
1 kg white sugar
1 litre water
1 stick cinnamon

Cut the stalks from the sour figs. Rinse the figs well and soak them overnight in the salted water. Drain the figs and rinse them in fresh water. Bring the sugar, water and cinnamon to the boil in a large, heavy-based saucepan and add the figs. Boil until the figs are shiny and the syrup is thick. Pack the jam into hot, dry, sterilized jars and seal.
Makes about 1.5 kg

NOTE: Dried sour figs can be used. Soak the figs overnight in water, then proceed as described above.

From left to right: Fresh Apricot Jam, Sour Fig Jam, Grape Jam and Ripe Fig Jam.

SLICED PEACH JAM

The first yellow cling peaches were imported from St Helena, and many a Boland and Karoo garden still boasts trees from this strain.

1 kg yellow cling peaches
60 ml salt dissolved in 5 litres water
100 ml water
1 kg white sugar
20 ml lemon juice

Halve, peel and stone the peaches. Soak them in salted water for a few hours to prevent discolouring. Drain. Slice the peaches 3–5 mm thick and place them in a large, heavy-based saucepan. Add the water and poach the peaches, covered, for about 10 minutes, or until just soft. Add the warmed sugar and lemon juice and stir until the sugar has dissolved. Boil, uncovered, until the peach slices are shiny and the syrup is thick. Pack in hot, dry, sterilized jars and seal immediately.
Makes about 1.5 kg

GRAPE JAM (KORRELKONFYT)

Large, juicy Hanepoot grapes make the best korrelkonfyt, my grandmother always said, but you can use any kind of grape to make this jam.

1 kg grapes, halved and seeded
750 g white sugar
20–25 ml lemon juice

Layer the grapes, sugar and lemon juice in a large, heavy-based saucepan and set aside for 2 hours, or overnight. Heat over low heat until the sugar has dissolved, then bring the mixture to the boil and boil over moderate heat until setting point is reached (see Testing if Jams and Jellies are Ready, page 120). Stir from time to time to prevent burning. Remove scum from the surface, if necessary, and pour the jam into hot, dry, sterilized jars. Seal immediately.
Makes 1 kg

QUINCE JELLY

Quinces make an excellent tart jelly, perfect for serving with roast meat like game, or using as a spread.

1 kg quinces
1.25 litres water
400 g white sugar per 500 ml juice

Place the quinces and the water in a large, heavy-based saucepan and bring to the boil over high heat. Reduce the heat and simmer gently for approximately 30 minutes, or until the quinces are tender. Mash the quinces against the sides of the saucepan occasionally, using a wooden spoon. Strain the quince pulp (see Straining the Juice, page 120). Discard the pulp once the juice has drained through completely. Measure the juice and return it to a large, clean, heavy-based saucepan. Add the sugar and stir the mixture over low heat until the sugar has dissolved. Bring to the boil. Boil rapidly, without stirring, until the jelly reaches setting point (see Testing if Jams and Jellies are Ready, page 120). Skim the foam from the surface, if necessary. Ladle the jelly into hot, dry, sterilized jars, leaving 1.2 cm headspace. Seal immediately.
Makes about 1 kg

VARIATION: Guava jelly may be prepared in the same way as quince jelly, but much less water is used for guava jelly. Use only 375 ml water per 1 kg guavas, and add 15 ml lemon juice per 500 ml juice.

From the top: Catawba Grape Jelly in the making, Apple Jelly and Quince Jelly.

APPLE JELLY

1 kg tart green apples
cold water
200 g white sugar per 250 ml juice
juice of 2 lemons

Chop the apples, skin and all, and place in a large, heavy-based saucepan. Add cold water to cover and bring to the boil. Boil until it is pulpy. Strain (see Straining the Juice, page 120). Measure the juice into a large, clean, heavy-based saucepan and add the warmed sugar and lemon juice. Bring to the boil and boil until setting point is reached (see Testing if Jams and Jellies are Ready, page 120). Skim, if necessary, and spoon into hot, dry, sterilized jars. Seal immediately.

Makes about 500 g

THREE-FRUIT MARMALADE

Marmalade, the British breakfast favourite, can be chunky or smooth, made from a single citrus fruit or from a combination. Sometimes other fruits are used, but there will always be some citrus fruit or juice in the mixture. South Africans enjoy marmalade much as the British do – as a spread with toast or bread. It can also be used in baking or in sauces served with pork or ham.

1 large orange, thinly peeled
1 large lemon, thinly peeled
1 grapefruit, thinly peeled
750 ml water per 250 ml minced fruit
200 g sugar per 250 ml minced fruit
5 ml glycerine

Wash the fruit, remove the pips and mince the fruit finely. Measure the fruit and place it in a large, heavy-based saucepan. Add the measured water and boil for 5 minutes. Add the sugar and heat over low heat, stirring occasionally, until the sugar has dissolved. Stir in the glycerine and boil rapidly until the marmalade reaches setting point (see Testing if Jams and Jellies are Ready, page 120). Pour into hot, dry, sterilized jars and leave to cool. Seal when cold.

Makes about 500 g

MICROWAVE OVEN: Place the prepared fruit and water in a large glass jug or deep bowl. Microwave, uncovered, at 100 per cent power for 10 minutes. Stir in the sugar and glycerine and microwave for about 18–20 minutes, stirring every 2–3 minutes. Leave the marmalade to stand for 10 minutes, then pour it into hot, dry, sterilized jars and seal when cold.

CATAWBA GRAPE JELLY

These tart grapes are delicious to eat, but the jelly they make is so good that you'll be tempted to use them only for that purpose.

2 kg catawba grapes
200 g white sugar per 500 ml juice
juice of ½ lemon

Wash the grapes well and pull them off the stalks. Place them in a large, heavy-based saucepan and bring slowly to the boil, shaking the saucepan often. Boil the grapes until the pips and skins float to the top. Strain (see Straining the Juice, page 120). Add the sugar and lemon juice and bring the mixture slowly to the boil, stirring often. Boil the mixture rapidly and test (see Testing if Jams and Jellies are Ready, page 120). Pour the jelly into hot, dry, sterilized jars and seal immediately.

Makes 1–1.5 kg

CHAPTER 12

PICKLES AND CHUTNEYS

Most nations have their own pickling recipes, mainly because in the days before refrigeration existed, it was just about the only way to preserve food for later use. Not only fruit and vegetables but also meat, fish and other protein foods were pickled – eggs, for example, and nuts like walnuts. The chutneys made in South Africa have a more pronounced flavour than most of those produced in Britain, Europe and the United States. This is mainly the legacy of the excellent Malay cooks who brought the more aromatic, spicier mixes to this country from the East. Chutneys can be fruity and mild, or hotter with the addition of chillies and other spices, but they are always thickish combinations of fruits and vegetables.

POTTING AND SEALING PICKLES

Fill clean jars – warm for cooked pickles – to within 2.5 cm of the top with pickles. If using raw vegetables, drain off any water that may gather at the bottom of the jar before adding the spiced vinegar. Cover the pickles with spiced vinegar – hot for cooked pickles and cold for raw pickles – to at least 1.5 cm over the vegetables. Vinegar evaporates during storage, and any pickle that is exposed will discolour. Cover and seal the jars, airtight, immediately.

POTTING AND SEALING CHUTNEYS

Pour the chutney into clean, warm jars while hot. Fill to within 1.5 cm of the top and cover tightly with airtight, plastic screw-on or pop-on lids, not metal ones, which will corrode from the action of the spices and vinegar. Leave to mature in a cool, dry, dark place for 6–8 weeks before use, or as directed in the recipe.

SPICED VINEGAR

Spiced vinegar is used as a preserving medium for many vegetable and fruit pickles.

1 litre white or brown vinegar
1 stick cinnamon
10 ml whole cloves
10 ml allspice berries
10 ml black peppercorns
10 ml mustard seeds
2–3 bay leaves

Place the vinegar and spices in a saucepan. Cover and bring to the boil, but do not allow to bubble. Remove from the stove and set aside for 2½–3 hours to infuse. Strain the vinegar into clean, dry jars and seal with plastic screw-on or pop-on lids.
Makes 1 litre

HERB VINEGAR

Herb vinegar is used as the preserving medium for Traditional Pickled Cucumbers (page 134).

200 g freshly gathered tarragon, sage, rosemary, mint, basil or other herb
750 ml white wine vinegar

Pick the herbs just before they flower. Wash the leaves and tender parts of the stalks. Place the herbs in a large clean jar and bruise them with a wooden spoon. Fill the jar with white wine vinegar, cover with a cloth and leave to steep for 2–3 weeks. (If using a clear glass jar, stand it in a dark cupboard to prevent colour loss.) Strain the vinegar through clean muslin into a clean jar. Place a fresh, washed sprig of the chosen herb in the jar and seal it with a plastic screw-on or pop-on lid. Leave to mature for 2–3 weeks before use.

TRADITIONAL PICKLED CUCUMBERS

These pickles came to South Africa with German settlers, where they became popular served with cold meats. Small, whole gherkins can be used instead of cucumbers.

2 kg pickling cucumbers
250 g salt
ice cubes
iced water
100 g white sugar
750 ml Herb Vinegar (above)
65 ml dill seeds
18 peppercorns

Wash and chop the cucumbers, or slice them thickly. Place them in a deep dish and sprinkle with the salt. Cover with ice cubes and iced water and set aside for 4 hours. Drain and rinse the cucumbers in cold water. Place the sugar and vinegar in a stainless-steel saucepan and stir to dissolve. Add the cucumbers and heat slowly to boiling point. Boil, uncovered, for about 5–6 minutes. Divide the dill seeds and peppercorns among six clean, warm jars, and then fill the jars with cucumbers and boiling vinegar. Seal immediately (see Potting and Sealing Pickles, above).
Makes about 3 kg

PICKLED BEETROOT

Sunday lunch was the time to bring out the pickled beetroot, said my grandmother, because it went so well with the roast meat and geelrys. These days, we serve pickled beetroot as a salad with cold meats or at a braai.

6 medium beetroot
200 g white sugar
1 litre white vinegar
250 ml water
3 small dried red chillies (optional)
1 star anise
6 black peppercorns

Wash the beetroot and cut off the leafy tops, without breaking the skin. Place them in a large saucepan of boiling water and simmer, covered, for 1 hour, or until the skins can be removed easily (or cook in a pressure cooker for about 30 minutes). Cool the beetroot, halve them and pack into clean jars. Combine the sugar, vinegar, water, chillies, star anise and peppercorns in a saucepan and simmer, stirring, until the sugar has dissolved. Cool and strain the liquid over the beetroot, covering them completely. Seal (see Potting and Sealing Pickles, page 134).
Makes about 1 kg

RAISIN PICKLE

A common sight on Boland farms, a few decades ago, were the beds of fruit like apricots, peaches and grapes drying in the sun. Raisins had many uses: to make yeast for baking, as a fermenting agent when making drinks like Pineapple Beer (page 140), as a baking ingredient, for adding to stewed fruit compôte, in chutneys and sauces, and also in this sweet and sour pickle.

250 g seedless raisins
200 g light brown sugar
250 ml brown vinegar
10 ml mustard seeds
2 ml milled black pepper
1 stick cinnamon
10 medium Traditional Pickled Cucumbers (page 134), drained and diced

Remove the stalks from the raisins, if necessary. Boil the sugar, vinegar and spices together for approximately 5 minutes. Add the raisins and cook until they are shiny and plump. Add the cucumbers and boil for about 5 minutes, then spoon the pickle into clean, hot jars and seal immediately (see Potting and Sealing Pickles, page 134).
Makes about 500 g

PICKLED RED CABBAGE

From top left: Herb Vinegar, Traditional Pickled Cucumbers, Raisin Pickle and Pickled Beetroot.

1 firm red cabbage
100–175 g coarse salt
450–600 ml white Spiced Vinegar (page 134)

Remove any discoloured leaves from the cabbage. Quarter the cabbage and wash it well. Remove the tough inner stalk and shred the cabbage. Layer the cabbage and salt in a basin, ending with salt. Leave for 24 hours. Rinse thoroughly in cold water and drain well. Pack into clean jars, cover with cold spiced vinegar and seal at once (see Potting and Sealing Pickles, page 134). Leave to mature for 1 week.
Makes about 2 kg

FRUIT CHUTNEY

Homesick South Africans living abroad generally put at the top of the list of things they miss a certain well-known brand of chutney. This recipe, while not purporting to be the original, comes quite close in flavour to a bottle of Mrs Ball's best.

200 g dried pears, chopped
200 g dried apricots, chopped
200 g dates, chopped
200 g dried apple rings, chopped
200 g sultanas
1 litre water
500 ml cider vinegar
400 g brown sugar
2 ml chilli powder
2 ml turmeric
2 ml freshly grated nutmeg
2 ml ground ginger
1 clove garlic, crushed

Place the fruit and water in a large bowl. Cover the bowl and leave overnight. Combine the undrained fruit mixture with the remaining ingredients in a large saucepan. Simmer over low heat, stirring, until the sugar has dissolved. Bring to the boil then simmer over low heat, uncovered, for about 1½ hours, or until thick, stirring occasionally. Pour into clean, warm jars and cool completely before sealing (see Potting and Sealing Chutneys, page 134).
Makes about 2 kg

MICROWAVE OVEN: Soak the fruit as described. Combine the fruit mixture with the remaining ingredients in a large bowl and microwave at 100 per cent power for about 40 minutes, or until thickened, stirring occasionally. Allow to cool completely before potting.

MANGO ATJAR

Fruit Chutney (left) and Mango Atjar, relishes of Malay tradition.

Relishes
Chutney, blatjang and atjar can all be classified as relishes, and although similar, they do differ in consistency. Chutney has a similar texture to that of jam, while blatjang is thinner. Atjar is more chunky in consistency and the different ingredients are more easily distinguishable.

Atjar, probably also introduced to this country by the Malays, consists of a variety of vegetables and fruits, boiled and preserved in a very strong chilli pickle. It should be pleasantly sour, with a sweetish aftertaste.

1.5 kg green mangoes, peeled, stoned and cut into 2 cm chunks
500 ml white vinegar
250 g white sugar
200 g blanched almonds, chopped
2 onions, sliced
60 ml chopped root ginger
5 ml cayenne pepper
5 ml mustard seeds
2 cloves garlic, crushed
5 peppercorns
5 ml salt

Boil all the ingredients until the mango chunks are tender, but still whole. Pour into clean, hot jars and seal (see Potting and Sealing Pickles, page 134).
Makes about 1.75 kg

APRICOT BLATJANG

Blatjang has a thinner consistency than chutney, and is generally hotter. A chopped red chilli can be added for those who really like to eat fire.

2 kg ripe apricots
1 large onion, chopped
1 clove garlic, crushed
500 g seedless raisins
400 g white sugar
1 ml cayenne pepper
5 ml salt
10 ml ground ginger
5 ml mustard powder
500 ml brown vinegar

Halve and stone the apricots. Mix all the ingredients in a stainless-steel saucepan and bring slowly to the boil. Simmer, uncovered, for 45 minutes to 1 hour, or until thickened, stirring occasionally. Pour into clean, warm jars and seal immediately (see Potting and Sealing Chutneys, page 134).
Makes about 3.25 kg

YELLOW PEACH PICKLE

Fruit pickles like this one illustrate perfectly the South African love of sweet and sour flavours.

3 kg yellow cling or loose-stone peaches, peeled, stoned and sliced
3 onions, sliced into rings
25 ml whole coriander seeds
15 ml peppercorns
10 ml allspice berries
1 piece root ginger
1.5 litres white vinegar
20 ml cornflour
25 ml curry powder
5 ml turmeric
10 ml salt
250 g white sugar

BRINE SOLUTION
100 g salt dissolved in 5 litres water

Soak the peaches and onions in the brine solution for 1 hour. Drain and rinse well in fresh water. Tie the spices and ginger in a piece of muslin. Place the muslin bag in the vinegar and bring to the boil. Mix the cornflour, curry powder, turmeric, salt and sugar to a paste with 30 ml cold water. Add to the vinegar, stirring constantly. Add the peaches and onions and boil, uncovered, for 10 minutes. Remove the bag and spoon the pickle into warm, clean jars. Seal immediately (see Potting and Sealing Pickles, page 134).
Makes about 4.5 kg

PICKLED ONIONS

Pickled onions are a popular relish in South Africa. If the onions are packed in cold vinegar, they will remain beautifully crisp during storage.

2.75 kg pickling onions
boiling water
1.5 litres Spiced Vinegar (page 134)

BRINE SOLUTION
1 kg coarse salt
10 litres water

First, make a brine solution by dissolving half the salt in half the water. Place the unpeeled onions in the brine solution, cover with a plate to keep the onions below the surface and leave them to soak for 12 hours. Drain the onions, place them in a large bowl and pour over enough boiling water to cover. Leave for 1 minute. Drain the onions, then top and tail and peel the onions. Prepare a second brine solution by dissolving the remaining salt in the remaining water. Leave the onions to soak in the brine solution, covered with a plate, for a further 24 hours. Remove the onions and drain them thoroughly. Pack the onions in clean jars, pour over the cold spiced vinegar and seal (see Potting and Sealing Pickles, page 134). Leave to mature for 6–8 weeks before use.
Makes about 3 kg

MICROWAVE OVEN: The onions can first be blanched in the microwave oven. Peel the onions, place them in a little water and microwave them at 100 per cent power for 1 minute. Place in the brine solution and continue as described in the recipe.

CHAPTER 13

FRUIT DRINKS, BEERS AND LIQUEURS

Fruit juices and syrups have always figured prominently in country catering, and South Africa is no exception. Among the local favourites are Apricot Juice (page 140) and Grape Juice (page 140). Fruit juices generally keep well, if properly stored, and make excellent gifts. Home-made beers can be made from hops, fruit, wheat – in fact almost anything you like – and all of them are incredibly potent. Liqueurs featuring fruit and brandy are an important part of our heritage. Van der Hum Liqueur (page 142) was developed here, as was buchu brandy. Fig leaves were often used as a base for liqueurs, especially if a greenish colour was required.

APRICOT JUICE

Among the more successful of Jan van Riebeeck's fruit tree 'transplants' from Europe were apricots, which took to the climate and soil with virtually no initial problems. It was the French Huguenots, however, who perfected cultivation methods. Apricots have a short harvesting season, starting with early varieties in December and ending in the middle of January, and the fresh fruit does not keep well. This is perhaps the most important reason that means were sought to preserve the bounty – apricots were used in chutneys, packed in brandy (see Boeremeisies, page 123) and also made into a juice.

apricots
500 ml water per 2 kg apricots
450 g white sugar per 2 litres juice

Wash and stone the apricots and weigh them. Calculate the quantity of water required. Place the apricots in a saucepan and add the water. Poach, covered, for about 20 minutes, or until soft. Purée the apricots and strain through muslin to obtain the juice. Measure the juice into a clean saucepan and calculate the quantity of sugar required. Add the sugar. Heat the fruit juice and sugar over low heat, stirring, until the sugar has dissolved. Strain into another saucepan. Bring the juice and sugar to boiling point, then pour it into sterilized bottles (see Sterilizing Jars for Preserves, page 120) and seal immediately.

PINEAPPLE BEER (PYNAPPELBIER)

Pineapple beer has become a part of the South African culinary tradition. Beware of this beer; it tastes like a cooldrink, but has the kick of a donkey.

skin of 1 large pineapple, chopped
7 litres lukewarm water
500 g white sugar, or to taste
75 ml raisins
10 ml active dry yeast

Wash the pineapple skin and rinse well. Mix the skin, lukewarm water, sugar and raisins in a large container. Sprinkle the yeast over and leave to stand for 30 minutes. Stir well, then cover with a clean tea towel and leave to mature for 24 hours in a cool place. Strain through muslin and bottle in sterilized bottles (see Sterilizing Jars for Preserves, page 120). Cap the bottles after 12 hours and use after 1–2 days.
Makes about 7 litres

NOTE: Chop the entire pineapple, not just the skin, for a more intense flavour.

GRAPE JUICE

Farmers' wives in the winelands and parts of the Karoo used some of the grape harvest to make grape juice for home consumption. The sweetness of the juice depended on the variety of grape used.

grapes
250 ml water per 4 litres pulp
white sugar (optional)

Remove the grapes from the stems, discard the pips and process the grapes in a food processor. Measure the pulp into the top of a double boiler and calculate the quantity of water needed. Add the water and heat over boiling water for 15 minutes. Strain through muslin and add white sugar to taste. Fill clean bottles with the juice, close and turn the lids back a quarter turn. Place on a trivet or an inverted plate in a large saucepan – deep enough to ensure that the bottles will be covered with water – with a tight-fitting lid. Make sure the bottles do not touch each other. Fill the saucepan with hot water until the lids are 5 cm under water. Cover the saucepan, bring the water to the boil and sterilize for 25 minutes at 90 °C (use a sugar thermometer). Remove the bottles with tongs, seal immediately and leave to cool.

LEMON SYRUP

In the past, virtually every home and farm garden had lemon trees. Many industrious housewives would make a supply of lemon syrup for later use. The Eureka lemon makes a tart syrup, but the Cape rough-skinned lemon is sweeter and produces copious quantities of juice.

ripe lemons
800 g white sugar per 1 litre juice

Squeeze the juice from the lemons and measure it into a saucepan. Calculate the quantity of the sugar required and add to the saucepan. Heat the juice over low heat, stirring, until the sugar has dissolved, but do not allow it to boil. Strain the mixture through muslin, then fill sterilized bottles (see Sterilizing Jars for Preserves, page 120). Seal immediately. To serve, dilute 1 part lemon syrup with 2 parts iced water or soda water. Add a sprig of mint for decoration. Lemon syrup will keep for up to 1 month in a cool, dry place.

GINGER BEER (GEMMERBIER)

Thirst-quenching ginger beer was ideal for the hot South African climate, which made it the favoured drink at Christmas-time in the 17th and 18th centuries, when the settlers had to get used to seasons that were reversed. It was also a popular drink at picnics.

4.5 litres water
30 g root ginger, crushed
500 ml white sugar
15 ml active dry yeast

Boil the water, then add the ginger and sugar. Remove from the stove and cool until lukewarm. Add the yeast and leave, covered, for 1–2 days. Strain the beer through muslin, bottle it in sterilized bottles (see Sterilizing Jars for Preserves, page 120) and seal. Refrigerate and serve chilled. Ginger beer will keep in the refrigerator for up to 1 week.
Makes about 4.5 litres

ORANGE LIQUEUR

Like so many of the early Cape liqueurs, orange liqueur is also based on brandy.

6 large oranges
500 g white sugar
5 ml ground cinnamon
2 ml ground coriander
1 litre brandy

Using a potato peeler, remove the rind from the oranges. Remove all the pith. Chop the rind finely. Squeeze the juice from the oranges and blend it with the sugar, cinnamon, coriander and rind. Pour into a large jar, then add the brandy and mix well. Cover the jar and leave the mixture to infuse for 2–3 months. Strain the liqueur through muslin into sterilized bottles (see Sterilizing Jars for Preserves, page 120). Seal and store. Orange liqueur will keep for many months in a cool, dry place.
Makes about 1.5 litres

From left: Grape Juice, Ginger Beer and Lemon Syrup, all refreshing traditional drinks.

VAN DER HUM LIQUEUR

This liqueur was named after Admiral van der Hum of the Dutch East India Company fleet who was fond of this nectar to the point of distraction.

6 whole cloves
1 stick cinnamon
½ nutmeg, grated
750 ml brandy
30 ml sliced naartjie peel
50 ml rum
250 g white sugar
125 ml water

Bruise the cloves and cinnamon and tie, with the nutmeg, in a muslin bag. Place the muslin bag, brandy, naartjie peel and rum in a sterilized jar (see Sterilizing Jars for Preserves, page 120) and cover. Leave in a cool place for 1 month. Shake gently every day. Strain the liqueur through muslin. Boil the sugar and water until very thick, then combine with the liqueur. Decant into dry, sterilized bottles and seal.
Makes about 1 litre

From left: Van der Hum Liqueur and Peppermint Liqueur are the ideal ending to a good meal.

PEPPERMINT LIQUEUR (JANGROENTJIE)

Peppermint liqueur has been made at the Cape since before 1800. The Dutch colonists would have used a fig leaf base instead of green food colouring to give the liqueur its characteristic green hue. The base was made by simmering young fig leaves in hot water until the water turned green and had a distinctive fig flavour. The juice was then strained and boiled with sugar, lemon juice and a pinch of salt to make a syrup.

250 g white sugar
250 ml water
500 ml brandy
3 drops peppermint essence
3 drops green vegetable colouring

Boil the sugar and water to make a thick syrup. Cool the syrup and add it to the brandy. Add the peppermint essence and green vegetable colouring. Bottle in sterilized bottles (see Sterilizing Jars for Preserves, page 120) and seal.
Makes about 750 ml

INDEX